FELICIA CARTRIGHT

AND THE
HONORABLE TRAITOR

Felicia   Joan

FELICIA CARTRIGHT

AND THE
HONORABLE TRAITOR

BERNARD PALMER

Cover Artwork: Adobe Firefly & Ideogram
Editor: Charlene Miskimen

Aneko Press Youth

www.anekopress.com

Aneko Press, Life Sentence Publishing, and our logos are trademarks of
Life Sentence Publishing, Inc.
203 E. Birch Street
P.O. Box 652
Abbotsford, WI 54405

JUVENILE FICTION / Religious / Christian / Action & Adventure

Paperback ISBN: 979-8-88936-310-1

eBook ISBN: 979-8-88936-311-8

10 9 8 7 6 5 4 3 2 1

Available where books are sold

CONTENTS

CHAPTER 1

DOORWAY TO THE PAST

Joan Bailey slipped behind the wheel of her red convertible and switched on the ignition. Usually she was the last to be ready. This afternoon, however, the slight, attractive dark-haired girl was the first one to the car and rattled her keys impatiently while she waited. Felicia Cartright went around to the other side and opened the door.

"So you finally decided to come." Joan's voice was serious, but her eyes danced merrily.

"Listen to her," Felicia countered, as though she were talking to some mythical third person. "Once in her life she gets here first, and she acts as though it's some major event – like being kissed by the queen."

"I'm simply following the example you and Becky set for me," Joan informed her. "I'm yipping at you the same as you two yip at me when you have to wait for a few seconds."

"A few seconds?" Felicia rolled her eyes in mock horror. "After all the time I've spent waiting for you!"

Joan colored slightly.

"Wipe that smirk off your face." She glanced down at her watch. "Did you tell Becky we wanted to leave right away?"

Felicia nodded.

"I saw her as I was coming out. She was going back to the room to get her notebook and a couple of pens – just in case."

"I don't think she'll need them," Joan murmured.

"Neither do I."

At that moment, Becky Strong came running up and opened the car door.

"I'm sorry I'm late," she panted, clambering in beside Felicia, "but I had to go back for my notebook."

"I hope you'll need it," Joan said cryptically. She started the engine and backed expertly out of the dormitory parking lot.

Leaves were falling, and the wind wore the biting edge of coming winter. Although it was not yet four, the sun was already low in the sky.

"You don't sound very optimistic," Becky replied, tossing her auburn hair out of her eyes. "What is it that Miss Duncan says? 'A Wellington girl is capable and self-assured – the equal to any situation.'"

"Only this is a little more than a situation. That's the trouble."

Felicia frowned curiously.

"You can say that again." She breathed deeply. "What makes this Miss Morrow so antagonistic, anyway? That's what I'd like to know."

Joan laughed.

"Didn't you hear Mrs. Graber yesterday afternoon when we tried to tell her how Miss Morrow has been avoiding us? 'Miss Morrow isn't antagonistic. She's just from solid New England stock. She's reserved and a rugged individualist.'"

"She's a rugged individualist, all right. I thought she was going to bite my head off when she came to the door the other day."

"You sound defeated already," Becky told her. "Miss Duncan would say that you have to expect success. Think positively."

"I'd like to have her give us a demonstration on old Miss Morrow," Joan said, her lips biting off the words. "Maybe she wouldn't be so confident after she had the door slammed in her face a few times."

"Miss Duncan just might be able to pull it off," Felicia observed. "She talks a lot about the ideal Wellington girl, and we act as though we get a little tired of it, but really, she comes close to being just that sort of person herself."

"I know." The banter left Joan's voice. "We don't want to give you a bum steer, Becky. Miss Duncan is a tremendous person. We do a lot of kidding about her and all of that, but it's just in fun. As a matter of fact, we all love her."

3

Becky nodded.

Although she had not been at Wellington School for Girls more than a few months, the stately, freckled redhead already sensed the respect the girls had for Miss Duncan.

"Why is Mrs. Graber so anxious that we interview Miss Morrow anyway?" she asked suddenly, changing the subject.

"That's what I've been wondering myself," Felicia said.

Joan turned at the next corner, paused until the signal light turned green, and headed for the little town of Stilwell, fourteen miles from Wellington.

"To quote Mrs. Graber," she said, "'Miss Morrow is from one of the oldest families in New England. If anybody would have fresh, unused material on Revolutionary War characters, she would.'"

Felicia opened her purse and searched for her lip gloss.

"I suppose you're right. But what I can't understand is why it should be such a big deal? Why does Miss Morrow have to be so difficult?"

* * *

One afternoon two or three weeks before, Miss Duncan had called the girls into her office.

"What does she want to see us about?" Becky asked fearfully.

"She didn't say." The girl's voice was cold and impersonal. "She just asked me to come and have you report to the office right away."

The newcomer turned, focusing on her companions. "Does she often call students in like this?"

"That depends," Joan said laconically. "If you conduct yourself as a model Wellington girl of character and integrity, get A's at all times, and don't slurp your soup, you may be able to avoid being called in for as long as a month."

Becky managed a thin laugh.

"You've got me scared already."

"I've been here for quite a while, and I'm always scared," the Bailey girl replied.

"We might just as well go down and get it over with." Felicia started for the door.

"Listen to her," Joan muttered. "If she was going to be executed, she'd want to be right on time just to 'get it over with.'"

The three girls went down to the dean's office on the first floor. The door was open, and they could see Mrs. Graber, their American History teacher, sitting across from Miss Duncan.

"Uh-oh," Joan muttered under her breath. "It must be history. And that's one subject I thought was safe."

"Come in, girls," Miss Duncan said, greeting them, "and close the door."

Joan eyed her uncertainly.

"Now what've we done?"

"I detect the workings of a guilty conscience," Miss Duncan replied without smiling. "The proper, well-bred Wellington girl does not jump to conclusions as you have done just now, Miss Bailey. She is sure of her conduct at all times. And because she knows she has conducted herself as a lady, she is not frightened half out of her wits because she has been called into the office."

Joan relaxed slightly. A faint smile tugged the corners of her mouth upward.

"As a matter of fact," the dean of women went on, "we haven't called you in because of anything you've done or haven't done. Quite the contrary."

The color came back into Becky's cheeks.

"You may not be aware of it, but Mrs. Graber has been working on a history project of sizeable proportions."

The instructor smiled self-consciously.

"I am writing a book on the Revolutionary War," she explained, "and I need help with it."

The girls stared.

"We don't know anything about writing a book," Joan blurted.

"I'll take care of the writing. It's the researching I'll need help on."

The girls stared at one another uncertainly.

"Since the three of you show such a marked interest in the Revolutionary period, Miss Duncan and I felt that you were the ones we should approach for help."

"It will mean extra credit, of course," the dean put in.

"Yes," Mrs. Graber said, "the school has very graciously agreed to allow extra credit for the project – if you are interested."

"Oh, we're interested all right." Felicia spoke quickly. "I wouldn't miss it for anything."

"I'm afraid you won't find the research very exciting," the history teacher continued. "You see, if I am to succeed, I'm going to have to uncover a great deal of previously unpublished material. I'm not content to do a rewrite of everything that's been done before. I want to unearth new material about little-known heroes of the period – material that will make a distinct contribution to our understanding of the era."

The phone rang, and Miss Duncan answered it.

"It sounds exciting," Felicia said softly.

"I can hardly wait to get started," Joan whispered under her breath.

After a moment or two, the dean hung up the phone.

"You girls will help Mrs. Graber?" she asked.

"Oh, we'd love to!" Felicia and Becky chorused.

"Fine. Mrs. Graber will be getting in touch with you in a few days."

Excitement danced in Felicia's eyes as they made their way back to their room.

"Doesn't that sound thrilling?" she asked.

"About as thrilling as sitting through one of Miss

Duncan's lectures on the qualities to be found in the ideal Wellington girl," Joan replied.

"I'm like Felicia," Becky exclaimed. "I'm so excited I can hardly wait to get started."

"Wait until they get you down at the historical library," Joan countered, "and you start going through those dirty, musty old records. You'll find out how exciting it is."

"Oh, I know that part of it will be dull, but just think. We'll be helping people to understand the period of the Revolutionary War a little better." She breathed deeply. "Future generations of Wellington girls might be reading the book we are helping with."

"Perish the thought!"

CHAPTER 2

RELUCTANT INFORMER

During the next several days, Mrs. Graber gave the girls elaborate instructions as to how they should go about gathering material and the sort of things to look for.

"I'm particularly interested in clues that will lead us to unknown people who should be recognized for their love of country and devotion to duty but aren't."

"And where will we find those clues?" Becky asked seriously.

Mrs. Graber smiled.

"If we knew the answer to that, we wouldn't have to do a great deal of research, Becky. You may find them in some diary that has been handed down from generation to generation. You may find them in an all but unknown journal at the historical library. Or you may find them referred to in the records of some of our older churches. That's why we've got to look in every conceivable place. We really don't know where we might stumble onto the leads that will make the book."

There was a short silence.

"I'd like to have you keep a record of the material you check, the people you visit, and the time you spend," she concluded. "All of those things will be factors in determining your extra credit."

"I knew there was going to be a catch to it," Joan murmured.

That night, the new project was all they could talk about.

"I'm so excited I can hardly wait to get started," Becky observed.

"So was I," Joan replied, "until she said we should start at the historical library."

"I thought I was going to burst right out laughing," Becky said. "You were certainly right when you said that she'd have us go there. It was the very first place she mentioned."

"Oh, I *knew* she'd be directing us there. Every time there's a term paper, Mrs. Graber sends us to the historical library. It must be an obsession of hers – or something."

"You'd think that anybody who was writing a book about the Revolutionary War would go to the historical library the first thing," Felicia said. "I don't see how she can expect us to find any new material in a place like that."

"We're supposed to be thumbing through those musty old pages looking for leads. Remember?"

"I guess she did say that we would probably be more apt to find the sort of material we're looking for in the homes of some of the older families around Wellington," Felicia went on. "And the old church records."

"I don't see how she expects us to find anything in old church records." Becky wrinkled her nose distastefully.

"I do," Felicia said.

Becky's blue eyes widened.

"You do?" she echoed curiously.

"Of course, I do. Some of the greatest heroes in the Revolutionary period were outstanding Christians. There could be mention of various church members in the church records that would give clues as to some of the things they did."

Becky went over and sat down. Briefly, her gaze traveled to the Bible on the nightstand beside Felicia's bed.

"I guess I haven't been able to see the importance of looking at church records because I've never seen the importance of religion," she said. "The way I look at it, it doesn't make any difference what you believe as long as you're sincere."

For the space of a moment or two, Joan was silent.

"That's interesting," she said, going over and picking up the Bible Becky had been looking at. "I believe this Bible is going to give me a lead on an authentic

Revolutionary War hero. I believe it so much I sit down and start reading every single word from page one through the book of Revelation. Will I find my hero?"

"Of course not," Becky retorted quickly.

"But I believe the man's name is there. I believe it with all my heart."

"It doesn't make any difference what you believe about that Bible. You won't find any war heroes in it."

"It doesn't make any difference what I believe, as long as I believe something."

"But we're not talking about religion now," Becky said testily. "We're talking about facts. And the fact is that that's a Bible, not a journal of 1770-1780."

Joan's voice was gentle when she replied.

"Why should we use a different standard for judging religion than anything else?" she asked. "As we do research for Mrs. Graber, we'll go to authentic documents of the period. We can consider nothing else. When we consider the faith we want to live and die by, we must do the same thing. We must go to the book of authority – the Word of God. And we can't put what we happen to believe against what the Bible says."

"You see, Becky," Felicia put in, "it doesn't make any difference what we believe about it. The Word of God has been – it is – and always will be."

Becky pursed her lips thoughtfully.

"If Mrs. Graber wants us to check old church records," she said at last, "I guess we can check them."

The next week or ten days the girls searched the historical library for material and went to several churches in the area to go through their records.

"I found out one thing," Joan said, throwing herself on the bed. "Most of it is just plain old-fashioned hard work."

"You can say that again," Becky complained. "I don't think I've ever been so tired in my life."

"At least Mrs. Graber didn't deceive us," Felicia said. "She warned us that the work wouldn't be very exciting."

Becky sat down on a chair near the bed and kicked off her shoes.

* * *

They had been at work a couple of weeks when they finally reached the stately white frame church at nearby Stilwell. The rector was a gentle, gray-haired man with a thin smile and watery eyes who had served the church more than forty years.

"Yes," he said, leaning forward and forming a church steeple with his long white fingers, "yes, we've got the records of our church since its founding in 1759."

"Would it be all right if we looked at them?" Felicia asked.

"I suppose so." He got to his feet. "You'll find them very dusty, I'm afraid."

* * *

"They're not only dusty," Becky complained some two hours later. "They're as dry as can be."

"About all they are is a list of the people who died or were married or had babies and had them christened," Joan said.

"There's a little more than that," Felicia said. "Listen to this. 'Uriah Morrow died August 17, 1789. Widow Morrow requested the rector to have the funeral. She also made request for permission to bury him in the church graveyard. After due consideration by the church board, both requests were denied. The rector was asked to make the decision of the board known to the widow Amelia Morrow.'"

"That doesn't sound like a hero to me," Joan said.

"Maybe not." Felicia's thin mouth tightened. "But I'd still like to find out what it's all about."

"It's probably an old drunk who threatened his wife and beat his kids," Joan said, "and the church board knew it."

Nevertheless, Felicia went to the rector's study.

"Yes," he said slowly in answer to her question. "The name Morrow is an old, illustrious name here in Stilwell. I think you would find there's always been a Morrow going to church here. The first meeting was held in the home of Ezekiel Morrow before there was a church building."

Felicia's eyes gleamed.

"That's most interesting. Where does the family live now?"

"Right here in Stilwell – all that's left of them." She whipped out her pen and notebook.

"Yes?"

"Miss Delphina Morrow is the only member of the family still alive." His face sobered. "It's a real tragedy having a proud name like Morrow disappear. It will be a sad day for the parish when Miss Delphina is laid to rest."

"Where does she live?"

"At the corner of Oak and Main. You see, the family came into hard times and had to sell the home quite a long while ago. Miss Delphina lives in a little cottage at Oak and Main."

"Alone?"

"I said she was the only one left in the family, and she didn't marry. Poor thing." Slowly his eyes widened. "You weren't planning on calling on her, were you?"

"As a matter of fact, we were," Joan put in. "Or I should say, Felicia is. She's just about to burst with curiosity."

"I'm afraid it won't do you any good. Miss Delphina doesn't see strangers. She lives alone – with her memories."

"It would be all right for us to try to see her, wouldn't it?"

"Oh, yes." He formed the church steeple with his

hands again. "Yes, I think it would be good. Miss Delphina just might decide to talk to three charming young ladies. At least it would be worth your trying."

They left the church and drove back to Wellington.

"I wish we had time to go and see Miss Morrow now," Felicia said.

"It doesn't sound to me as though it's going to take very long to see her," Joan put in. "She probably won't even come to the door."

Felicia scarcely heard her.

"Miss Delphina Morrow sounds like a very unhappy person to me."

There was a short silence.

"You know," Joan said as they neared the school once more, "what the rector said doesn't square with what we found in the church record."

"About the Morrow family being so upright?" Becky asked. "I was just thinking about that. It doesn't sound as though this Uriah Morrow was such a good character."

"Any family can have its black sheep."

"At least you've got to give them credit," Joan said. "Illustrious family or not, they believed in discipline. They certainly gave the back of the hand to Uriah Morrow. They didn't let that stop them."

Felicia sat in silence for several minutes.

"That's true, in a way," she said at last. "But it seems strange to me that there wasn't any previous record of Uriah Morrow before his death."

"Oh, he was probably recorded in the births and christenings," Becky retorted. "I skimmed over a lot of them."

"That's not what I meant." She brushed at her hair with a quick, impulsive gesture. "Apparently he did something so bad they didn't want their minister to conduct the funeral and wouldn't even let his body be buried in their cemetery. But there was no reference to discipline while he was alive."

"Maybe they didn't do that," Becky said.

"Maybe not – but it still seems strange to me."

The next afternoon, as soon as classes were finished, the girls drove back to Stilwell and located Miss Morrow's cottage.

"She has a lovely little home," Felicia murmured as they got out.

"And such beautiful flowers."

"You wouldn't think a person who loves flowers as much as she does would be so difficult to talk to, would you?"

"We'll soon know," Joan said.

She knocked on the door.

No answer.

"Maybe she isn't home," Becky ventured.

"The rector said she's always home." Joan knocked again.

After a minute or so, the girls heard a door inside open and close.

"She must be coming," Felicia whispered.

"Either that or she thinks we've gone."

Before Becky or Felicia had time to speak, the lock snapped, and the door creaked open an inch or two. They could see one mild blue eye, a nose, and part of a mouth and chin. The rest of the figure was hidden behind the door.

"Well?" she shrilled.

Joan gasped.

"What do you want?"

"We—we'd like to talk to you."

"I don't know you. I've never seen you before." With that she slammed the door. The lock clicked metallically.

CHAPTER 3

FELICIA'S ENTRÉE

Briefly, Felicia and her companions remained motionless on the steps of the Morrow cottage.

"Well," Joan exclaimed when she could speak, "what do you make of that?"

"I don't think she's very anxious to have company," Felicia said.

"The rector, or minister, or whatever you call him was certainly right," Becky put in. "She isn't very friendly."

"That," Joan replied, "is the understatement of the year."

"What are we going to do now?" the new girl wanted to know.

"It's not going to do any good to stand here talking. That's for sure." Joan started back to the car. "She's not going to come to the door."

"I wonder why."

Joan shook her head.

"There you go again. I don't know why you have to be so curious. Why can't you be like Becky and me? We decide Miss Delphina is a bit strange and let it go at that. But not you. You've got to keep wondering about it."

"There must be a reason for her to act that way," Felicia said.

"The next thing you'll be telling us is that you feel sorry for her."

The Cartright girl's soft blue eyes focused on Joan.

"As a matter of fact, I do feel sorry for her."

"I knew it." She gestured quickly with one hand. "I knew it. Here we go again."

"Now you're just as interested in Miss Morrow as I am."

"The difference is that I know when I'm licked, and you don't. You'll keep fussing and stewing about her for a month."

Mrs. Graber called the girls in to talk with them the next day.

"I've been looking over your records," she said. "You've been doing a tremendous amount of work. I want you to know that I appreciate it."

"The only trouble is that we've lost out on the best lead we've had," Joan said. "Miss Delphina Morrow won't talk to us."

"That's too bad. I've been hearing about the Morrow family. They're one of the oldest families in Massachusetts."

"Any help she's got for your book is going to die with her," Joan said. "She's not going to talk to anyone."

But Felicia was not so sure.

"I can't help thinking that she'll talk to us if we can just get acquainted with her. She must be very lonely."

"If she's lonely, she's going to stay that way."

"I'd like to go see her again," Felicia said. "Anyone who can grow flowers like she does can't be such a recluse as all that." Her young face softened. "She acted as though she's afraid of something, it seems to me."

"I wouldn't know whether she would ever talk to you or not," the history teacher said, "and even if she does, she might not have any material that would do me any good. But I would appreciate it if you would follow through as best you can. There is a possibility that she could make a very important contribution to my book."

Joan shrugged.

"Okay. I guess it won't hurt to get the door slammed in our faces again."

That night, before going to bed, Joan and Felicia had their devotions together as they always did in the evening. Becky sat at her desk studying.

"Don't forget to pray about going to see Miss Morrow tomorrow," Felicia said.

Becky looked up quickly.

"Do you think that will do any good?" she demanded curiously.

"Of course. God tells us in the Bible that He wants us to pray."

"About a little thing like that?"

"He says that He wants us to pray about everything."

The Cartright girl would have said more, but Becky had already turned back to her books.

Felicia could think of little else as she went to classes the next day. She had a surprise quiz in English that morning, and she knew she did miserably on it. How could she help it when all she could think of was Miss Delphina Morrow who hid herself behind the door of her inviting little cottage?

At last, school was over, and she was riding to Stilwell with Joan and Becky.

"What do we do?" Joan asked. "Draw straws to see who puts her head on the chopping block?"

"Why don't we all go up the way we did the last time?"

"I can see the headlines now," Joan continued. "Three Wellington girls missing. Last seen approaching the cottage of Miss Delphina Morrow in Stilwell."

"Joan!" Felicia scolded. "Don't talk like that."

She sighed in resignation.

"If that's the way it's got to be, all right. If you insist on taking Becky and me along with you to your doom, there's nothing we can do about it."

She pulled up to the small white cottage and stopped.

"If you're afraid to go with me, I'll go alone," Felicia said.

"Oh, no. We've been friends too long to be separated now. We'll go with you."

At the door once more, Felicia knocked lightly.

No answer.

"She's not going to come to the door," Joan said. "I can tell you that right now."

Felicia rapped again.

All was silent.

"I thought God was going to answer your prayer about getting to see Miss Morrow," Becky said.

At that instant, there was a sharp crashing sound inside.

"What was that?" Joan cried.

Felicia tried the door instinctively. It was locked.

"Meow!"

The girls laughed nervously.

"Miss Delphina must have a cat," Becky observed.

"He must be a very clumsy cat," Joan said.

"Listen!" Felicia whispered.

"What do you hear?"

"She's in there. I can hear her walking."

"What good's it going to do for us to know she's inside?" Joan asked. "She's not going to answer the door. That's for sure."

Felicia knocked again before turning reluctantly toward the street.

"I was so in hope that she'd come to the door," the Cartright girl murmured.

In spite of herself, Joan giggled.

"Now, what was that for?"

"I couldn't help it. You've been so sure you were going to get in to talk with Miss Morrow this afternoon."

"There's not much chance of it now."

They went back to the car and were just driving away when Felicia grasped Joan by the arm.

"Joan!" she cried. "Stop! Stop the car!"

She jammed on the brakes. The sleek convertible lurched to a stop. Only then did she glance around blankly.

"What was that all about?" she demanded.

"I want to get that kitten."

"It won't do you any good," Becky told her. "You can get him, but you can't take him into the dorm. That was one of the first things Miss Duncan told us in orientation. No pets of any kind."

"I'm not going to take him home."

"Then what are you going to do with him?"

Felicia did not reply until she caught the bedraggled, hungry-looking kitten and came back.

"Joan, drive around the block and park where Miss Morrow can't see the car and wait for me."

"What's this all about?"

"I think I've got a way of getting into the house, that's all."

"With a kitten?"

"With a kitten."

Felicia left her companions and walked slowly up

the walk to the Morrow cottage, holding the kitten in her arms. Miss Morrow must have been watching. She opened the door almost immediately.

The door was not open wide, but Felicia could see that Miss Morrow was no taller than she was, a slender wisp of humanity, gray of hair and wrinkled of face, but surprisingly spry. Her dress was clean and crisp, and she wore it with a dignity that seemed to lend beauty to it, although it was only faded cotton.

"Hello," Felicia said, smiling as brightly as she knew how.

"What do you want?"

Miss Morrow was talking to Felicia but staring curiously at the kitten the girl was holding.

"We saw this kitten out in the street," Felicia said. "The poor thing looked so forlorn and hungry. I stopped and picked him up."

"Well?" Miss Morrow still sounded cold, almost belligerent.

"We can't take him back to school with us. There's a regulation against having pets in the dorm."

The door opened a little wider.

"I thought I might get you to give him some milk."

"He does look hungry, doesn't he?"

"He looks as though he's about starved."

Miss Morrow flung the door open wide.

"Won't you come in?"

Felicia stepped into the living room and closed the door behind her.

The room was small and sparsely furnished with early American furniture that had a worn, authentic look about it. The drapes at the plate glass window were heavy and forbidding – the kind that could exclude every stray beam of light. And the lamps produced such a dim light that it seemed they were still using the kerosene they had been originally designed for.

Miss Morrow took the kitten from Felicia's arms and cradled him lovingly.

"Please excuse me, and I'll get the kitty some milk," she cooed. "You'll like that, won't you, Kitty?"

Once she was alone, Felicia moved to the center of the room and looked around. The rug was threadbare in places, like the rug in her grandmother's home. On the wall hung a large painting of a handsome young man in the nondescript uniform of the Continental Army.

It was a modest home, she could see at a glance. But it was an inviting, comfortable room for all of that – the sort of room that whispered of happy voices and a hymn sing around the piano.

Miss Morrow was only gone a few minutes. When she finally came back, the muscles around her mouth were relaxed slightly.

"Kitty is finishing his milk," she explained. "You never saw such a hungry little fellow."

"Thank you for feeding him." Felicia's smile was reassuring.

"I'm the one who should thank you for bringing him to me." For the first time she smiled, feebly, as though she were unaccustomed to smiling. "Of course, Timothy B – he's my cat–Timothy B is very jealous. But I called him out on the porch and talked to him. I said, 'Timothy B, this is the way I took you in when you were cold and hungry, so don't be so angry with this kitty.'"

She sat down, sighing deeply.

"Now I shall have to name him, and that's always such a bother."

"Why don't you call him Patches?" Felicia suggested. "He's got a patch of black over one eye."

"Patches?" Miss Morrow echoed. "I couldn't do that. Timothy B would never have anything to do with him if he had such an undignified name. I don't mean to talk about Timothy B, but he is actually quite a snob. Would you believe it? There are only two or three cats in this entire neighborhood that he will have anything to do with."

The girl murmured something under her breath. A few moments later, she glanced at her watch.

"Oh, it's later than I thought. I must be running along. We eat dinner at 6:30 at the school."

Miss Morrow followed her to the door.

"I don't believe I recall your name," the older woman said.

"I'm Felicia Cartright."

"I'm so glad to know you, Felicia. You may call me Miss Delphina if you like. That's what my friends have always called me."

"Thank you."

"You may stop back any time you're in the neighborhood to see how the kitty is doing, Felicia."

"I'd like that."

Back at the car, Becky and Joan were eagerly waiting for her.

"How did you make out?"

"What took you so long?" Joan wanted to know. "We were about to get the police."

"It's a long story." Felicia laughed.

"It must be." Joan started the engine and pulled slowly away from the curb.

"What did she have to say?"

"What's she like?"

"Is she going to help with material for Mrs. Graber's book?"

"Wait a minute," Felicia exclaimed. "I'll try to answer your questions one at a time."

Starting with Miss Delphina opening the door, she related all that had taken place.

"She sounds like some sort of a kook to me," Joan said. "Talking to a cat as though he's a real person."

"I think that's just a habit she's gotten into because she's been so lonesome living alone. Really, she seems like quite a nice person."

"But what about the book?" Becky demanded. "Is she going to help with it?"

Felicia's eyes widened.

"I don't know. I completely forgot to ask her about it."

CHAPTER 4

ABRUPT DISMISSAL

Felicia wanted to go back to see Miss Delphina the next day, but she had so many studies that it was impossible. It was the first of the following week before she was able to get away. She borrowed Joan's car and drove over to Stilwell to talk with Miss Delphina once more. She thought she was going to have to go alone, but Becky stopped her as she was leaving the dorm.

"Are you going over to see Miss Morrow this afternoon?" she asked.

Felicia nodded.

"Alone?"

"Joan was going with me, but at the last minute she found out she has to make up an English paper, so she couldn't."

"I thought I was going to have to work in the library this afternoon," Becky continued, "but I was able to get someone to take my place." From beneath lowered eyelids, she studied the other girl's features. "So I can go with you. That is, if you don't think I'd be in the way."

"I'd love to have you."

Miss Delphina came to the door in response to Felicia's knock. A frown chased the smile from her lips as she saw Becky.

"Hello." She did not open the door wide enough for them to go in.

"Hello, Miss Delphina." The Cartright girl's smile was gracious and friendly. "This is a good friend of mine, Becky Strong."

"I thought you'd be alone," she retorted, her tone reserved, almost injured.

"I was afraid I'd have to come alone, but Becky was good enough to ride with me."

"I see." A faint smile came to her mouth briefly. "Won't you come in?"

Becky followed Felicia into the living room and sat down beside her on the couch. Miss Delphina minced across the room and sat across from them.

"I was beginning to wonder whether you were ever going to come back or not."

"I wanted to come right away," Felicia explained, "but you know how it is when there are lessons to get. I just didn't have a minute."

Once more silence reigned.

"And how is the kitty?" the girl asked.

"You mean Jonathan Cartright?" Miss Delphina

eyed her wistfully. "I took the liberty of naming him after you," she explained.

"How nice."

"I thought you would like that. You were so concerned about Jonathan Cartright when you brought him here I thought it would be nice to have a remembrance of your kindness."

"How is he?"

Miss Delphina's face fell.

"He ran away. I think he was hurt that Timothy B didn't accept him as one of the family." Her voice raised. "You can be sure I scolded Timothy B good and proper for it. I told him it wasn't very gracious of him to treat Jonathan Cartright so shamefully. But you shouldn't feel too harsh toward Timothy B. I think he was J-E-A-L-O-U-S of Jonathan."

"At least Jonathan got a good meal and a warm place to stay for one night."

"Yes, it is too bad he wouldn't stay with us. I know it wouldn't have been long until Timothy B treated him like one of the family."

Felicia and Becky talked about Miss Delphina's antique furniture and the beautiful flowers she raised. It wasn't long until the older woman was visiting with them easily.

"I suppose you're wondering why we came to see you in the first place," Felicia said at last.

"To bring me Jonathan Cartright, wasn't it?"

"Before that, I mean."

Miss Morrow's expression changed slowly. The light in her eyes went out, and the frown muscles around her mouth tightened.

"You weren't one of those disgraceful girls who came hammering on my door, were you?"

"I didn't think we were disgraceful, Miss Delphina," Felicia countered. "But I was one of the girls who knocked on your door."

"I'm sorry I used that word," Miss Delphina said stiffly, "but I am shocked and hurt. I thought you came because of your concern for poor little Jonathan Cartright. Now I find you had some selfish motive. And I was just beginning to like you."

"I was concerned about Jonathan," Felicia said, "and it wasn't a selfish motive that brought us. We came in an effort to help somebody else."

"Yes?" Miss Delphina was still not completely convinced.

"One of our American History teachers is writing a book on the Revolutionary War and–"

"I may be old," she broke in primly, "but my memory doesn't go back quite *that* far."

Becky giggled in spite of herself. Miss Delphina was still serious, but her eyes danced.

"Mrs. Graber wants to write a book about Revolutionary War personalities who haven't been widely known but ought to be."

"And what does that have to do with me?" the older woman demanded.

"We thought perhaps you would have some material that had not been published before," Felicia went on. "Something about your ancestors who fought in the war, perhaps." She indicated the picture on the wall behind her and Becky with a jerk of her head.

"I'm afraid not." There was a note of finality in her voice.

Felicia tried to mask her disappointment.

"This painting is of one of your ancestors, isn't it?" she asked.

Miss Delphina nodded reluctantly.

"My great-great-great-grandfather," she said. "But he lived a long time ago."

Becky and Felicia turned to study the painting.

"He was handsome, wasn't he?"

Pride crept into the old woman's voice.

"All the Morrow men were handsome."

"It would be nice to have the story of at least one of them in Mrs. Graber's book."

Briefly, interest gleamed in Miss Delphina's faded blue eyes.

"Yes," she murmured, "no story of the Revolutionary period of this area could be complete without mention of the Morrows."

"Then you'll help us?" the Cartright girl asked excitedly.

"I'm sorry, Felicia," she replied curtly. "But I have nothing."

The girls rose to leave.

"Thank you, Miss Delphina," Becky said, extending her hand.

"If you should come across any material that would be helpful," Felicia reminded her, "would you please call me at the Wellington School for Girls?"

Miss Delphina's eyes widened.

"Wellington?" she echoed. "Do you girls attend Wellington?"

"I thought you knew that."

"How would I know you go to Wellington?" Her hands fluttered nervously. "My goodness, all the Morrow young ladies have gone to Wellington."

"Are you a Wellington grad?"

Miss Delphina's smile fled.

"All except me," she acknowledged. Bitterness crept into her voice. "There were some unfortunate circumstances when I was a young lady that made it impossible for me to go there. It was the biggest disappointment of my life."

"That's too bad."

"I'm going to look around here," she said. "There's a bare possibility that I might be able to come up with something that would be of help to your Mrs. Graber."

"Oh, that would be wonderful."

"I'm not promising, mind you."

She followed the girls to the door, still talking about Wellington. As they were about to leave, she changed the subject abruptly.

"How did you girls come to choose me to talk with?"

"Mrs. Graber had been hearing that your family was one of the oldest in the area," Felicia said. "But

I think the real reason was that Becky and Joan and I found the Morrow name mentioned in the records of the Stilwell Church."

At the mention of the church, Miss Delphina stiffened.

"We Morrows have not been churchgoers," she said.

"But I thought–" Felicia exclaimed before she realized what she was saying and checked herself.

"You thought what, Felicia?"

"It was just a remark the rector made when we were talking to him. It was nothing."

"And what did he say?" she demanded, bristling.

"I don't even remember for sure now," Felicia answered lamely. "But whatever it was, I got the impression that you were an active member of the congregation."

"Not at all." She bit the words into one syllable segments. "I was christened in the church and was taken into membership when I was twelve years old – against my own wishes I assure you. My mother made me go through with that ordeal, but I haven't been back since, except when I felt I had to. But the rector keeps my name on the church rolls and comes around visiting once a year – or at least he used to until I quit going to the door – and asks for my offering."

Her eyes flashed.

"No, I would not say that I'm an active church member."

"I'm sorry," Felicia said gently.

"That I feel that way about the church? I'm just being realistic – unhypocritical."

"I'm sorry you feel that way about God," Felicia told her. "You know, He loves you."

Miss Delphina seemed surprised that the girl would say what she had.

"I've never seen any evidence of it," she retorted defensively.

"He loves you so much He sent His Son to die on the cross so you can be saved and go to heaven."

An awkward silence stood between them.

"I'm sorry," the older woman said icily, "but it's almost time for dinner, and Timothy B gets so sulky if I keep him waiting. You'll excuse me, won't you?"

"Of course." The Cartright girl smiled. "You'll call if you find anything that would help Mrs. Graber, won't you?"

The frown lines deepened about Miss Delphina's face.

"I've been thinking it over," she answered. "I'm sure that I have nothing that would interest her."

With that she gestured toward the door, indicating that the visit was over.

Felicia and Becky stepped out into the gloom of the early winter evening.

"That was a revolting development," Becky observed.

At the car, Felicia stopped momentarily. "I wonder why she's so bitter about the church."

CHAPTER 5

MISS DELPHINA COOPERATES

Felicia and Becky were entering the dormitory after driving back from Stilwell when a girl who worked in the office met them.

"Oh, there you are. I've been looking all over for you."

"We had permission to leave the campus," Becky said quickly.

"A phone call came for you a little while ago, Felicia," the girl said. "You're to call this number."

Felicia glanced at the number. "Did the person leave a name?"

"No." She shook her head. "She just said that I was to give you this number as soon as you got in and tell her to call her at Stilwell. She said it was most important."

"Miss Delphina?" Becky asked.

"She's the only one in Stilwell I know," the Cartright girl answered, "but I can't see why she would call me."

"Maybe Jonathan Cartright has come back, and she wanted to call and tell you that Timothy B was glad to see him."

Felicia called the number that had been left for her.

"This is Miss Delphina," the shaking voice said. "I'd like to talk with you as soon as possible, Felicia."

"I'm afraid I won't be able to come out tonight. We're not allowed to go out of town on weeknights."

"I see." Disappointment thickened her voice. "Can you come over the first thing in the morning?"

"I have classes until after three," Felicia said. "But we'll come just as soon as they are over."

"I'll be looking for you. And do bring that sweet Becky person with you."

"I'd like to bring another girl along too, if I may." Miss Delphina hesitated.

"Is she a friend of yours?"

"A very good friend."

"I suppose it will be all right."

* * *

Miss Delphina met Felicia and her companions on the porch.

"I'm so glad you came," she fluttered.

Felicia saw that she had put on a different dress and was wearing an exquisite cameo on a slender black ribbon around her neck.

She ushered them into the house and had them sit down.

"The tea will be ready in a moment. I put the water on the stove when I saw you drive up."

The girls looked at one another and then at their hostess.

"You wanted to see us?" Felicia asked at last.

"Yes." She folded her dainty, work-worn hands in her lap. "Yes, I wanted to talk to you."

Before she could continue, there was a faint meowing at the door.

"Don't pay any attention to that," she said primly. "I have had to punish Timothy B today. He's been sulking again."

Joan snickered.

"Is there something wrong, my dear?"

Joan shook her head, her cheeks deepening in color.

"I–I'll be all right."

"What was it you wanted to see us about?" Felicia asked, changing the subject.

"Oh, yes." Miss Delphina's eyes narrowed. "Yes, I did call you, didn't I?"

"You said it was something important."

The older woman nodded.

"It is something important – most important. I think I am going to be able to help you with material for the book after all."

"You are!" they chorused.

"There's an old trunk in the attic. I haven't looked

in it for sixty years. But it used to have some mementos of the Morrow family's early days in America."

"Oh, that's wonderful!"

"Perhaps you had better wait until you've gone through it," she continued. "There may not be anything in it that would help your history instructor with her book."

"I'm sure there will be," Joan said. "Your family has been here for so long and has been so active in the affairs of the country."

Miss Delphina's expression changed slightly. The muscles at the corners of her mouth tightened, and steel glinted in her eyes.

"Yes, of course," she said coldly. She got to her feet and made her way painfully into the bedroom. "I also found this," she said, laying an old scrapbook on Felicia's lap. "My father put this together years ago. I don't know whether there's anything in here that will do you any good though. You can take it back to the school with you if you'd like."

"Thank you."

"And the same with anything you find in the trunk. I'd like to have you take good care of anything you take from here so I'll be sure to get it back when you're finished, but you can take it with you and keep it as long as your Mrs. Graber needs it."

"Oh, thank you. She'll appreciate that a great deal."

It was too late for the girls to go to the attic and examine the trunk that afternoon, so they made arrangements to see it the next time they could get to Stilwell.

"Just come anytime," Miss Delphina said. "I'm always home."

"Thank you. We'll do that."

"And Felicia," Miss Delphina said when they were leaving, "I would appreciate it a great deal if you would keep my remarks about the church a little secret between us."

"We won't say anything to anyone about it."

"I knew I could trust you. We Morrows have been such important people in New England that the rector likes to tell people I am a member of his church, as though I'm heartily behind him and the things he's doing. I'm afraid it would hurt him deeply if I let him know exactly how I feel."

"It isn't what we think about the church that makes the difference," Felicia reminded her. "It's what we do with the person of Jesus Christ."

Miss Delphina focused narrowly on her.

"That's the second time you've said something strange about religion."

"It isn't strange at all," Felicia answered. "It's what the Bible says. *All have sinned and come short of the glory of God.* That means you, me, every person in the world."

Miss Delphina winced.

"But God doesn't stop there. If He did, there wouldn't be any hope for any of us. The Bible says,

The wages of sin is death, but the gift of God is eternal life through Jesus Christ, our Lord."

She breathed deeply.

"That means that even though we are all sinners and have earned death and hell, God made a provision for us to escape it. He sent His Son, Jesus Christ, to die on the cross so we can confess our sin and put our trust in Him to save us."

Miss Delphina bristled.

"You are not talking with a skid-row character, Felicia," she retorted testily. "You are talking with a Morrow. I'll have you know that we are not like so many others. We are an honorable, upright family."

She reached for the door.

"You may come back to look through the trunk at your leisure."

Out in the car, Felicia opened the scrapbook and looked at it.

"This seems to be mostly old newspaper clippings," she observed. "And they don't go back so far either."

But Becky was not interested in the scrapbook at the moment.

"I thought you were going to upset things with Miss Delphina by talking to her about religion, Felicia," she said. "She was getting mad."

"I didn't want to say anything to offend her," the Cartright girl replied, "but I had to let her know that she's got to make a decision for Christ if she's going to go to heaven."

Becky turned in the seat.

"Now, Felicia," she countered, "you don't mean to tell me that God would send a sweet, dear old lady like Miss Delphina to hell, do you?"

"The Bible tells us that there is only one way to get to heaven. That's by confessing our sin and putting our trust in Jesus Christ to save us. It doesn't exclude anyone, so it has to mean Miss Delphina too."

Becky thought about that momentarily.

"Well," she said at last, "if that's the way things are, I suppose it means me too."

She tried to sound flippant, but the words didn't come out that way.

That night in their room, the girls pulled their chairs together and pored over the scrapbook.

"It's got a lot in it about the Morrow family," Joan said, "but there's not much about the Revolutionary War period."

Becky turned the page.

"What's this?"

Felicia read the inked receipt aloud. "'Received from Mrs. Amelia Morrow, payment in full for one gravestone for Uriah Morrow, September 19, 1790. Signed. Sebastian Haines.'"

"Even if the church board didn't think much of this Uriah character, his widow must have," Joan said, laughing. "First she wanted the minister to preach his funeral. Then she asked permission to bury him in the church graveyard. Finally, she bought a stone for him."

Felicia read the item again.

"Makes me wonder where they buried him," she said.

"Now, wait a minute," Joan exclaimed. "If you think you're going to get me out in some old cemetery trying to find a grave that's been there over two hundred years, you'd better think again. That's where I draw the line."

* * *

The next afternoon the girls went back to the little cottage to see Miss Morrow. She led them to the attic and switched on the light.

"I'm sorry, but I'll have to go to the meat market, so I won't be able to stay here with you this afternoon," she said. "Timothy B has been most unhappy with his liver and fish lately. I must go down and talk with Mr. Shultz about it."

"What should we do if you're not back when we have to leave?" Felicia wanted to know.

"Turn the latch on the door and pull it shut. I'll have the key with me."

The girls sat on the floor around the opened trunk and began to go through the contents. There was a crude hunting knife with a bone handle, an old medicine book, and some small pewter cups of uncertain design.

"Doesn't look as though there's much in here, does it?" Joan asked.

"There might be an interesting history to some of these things," Felicia put in, "if we just knew what it was."

Becky looked at her watch.

"We've got to run, or we'll be late for dinner again."

"And that'll never do," Joan added. "I'm starved."

She looked down at the trunk.

"Do you think it will do any good to come back?" she asked, discouraged.

"You've heard about the prospector who would have found a million dollar gold mine if he'd just turned over one more shovelful of earth, haven't you?" Felicia asked, laughing.

"I suppose that's supposed to mean something profound like, 'let's keep at it,'" Joan said. "But right now, I'm too tired to care."

Miss Delphina was still not back, so they locked the door behind them and went out to the car. Joan looked around uneasily.

"Felicia," she said, keeping her voice down. "Do you remember seeing that car across the street when we came this afternoon?"

The Cartright girl shook her head.

"I think it was there," Joan went on. "I remember it distinctly. There were two men sitting in it."

"What's so strange about that?"

They drove away slowly.

"Maybe nothing. But I've got the uneasy feeling that they've been watching us."

"Why would anyone want to watch us?" Becky asked curiously.

"I don't know." Fear laced Joan's voice. "And I don't know why they'd want to follow us, either, but they sure are!"

"What?"

"They're following us. They just made a U-turn and are coming up behind us!"

"You're kidding!" Becky cried.

"If you don't believe me, take a look!"

CHAPTER 6

LOVE LETTERS

Felicia scooted over so she could look in the rear-view mirror.

"They are behind us, Joan," she acknowledged. "But that doesn't necessarily mean they're following us."

"I'll show you."

Joan swung around the next corner. The car behind them followed.

"See, what'd I tell you?" she asked triumphantly. "They're following us, all right."

"Turn again and see if they still follow us," Felicia suggested.

The dark late-model car turned again, keeping the same distance behind them.

"Are you satisfied now?" Joan asked, her voice breaking fearfully. "Or do you still think it's just a coincidence?"

"Maybe it's some boys following us," Becky

suggested. "They do that around our hometown once in a while just for kicks."

"But we're not in your hometown," Joan said. "We're proper, well-bred Wellington girls. And besides, those aren't boys back there." Her voice lowered to a hoarse whisper. "They're men!"

"Why would anyone want to follow us?" Felicia asked. "All we've been doing is going through a trunk that belongs to an innocent, strange-acting old lady."

"There's got to be *some* reason for it."

"If they *are* following us," Felicia suggested.

Out on the highway, the girls lost track of the car they suspected was following them. And by the time they reached the school, they had all but forgotten it.

They wanted to go back to Stilwell the next afternoon to finish going through the Morrow trunk, but a savage snowstorm ripped in from the mountains, and it was three days before Joan even thought about using her car.

"Think we can get over to see Miss Delphina this afternoon?" Felicia asked her at lunch.

She pursed her lips thoughtfully. "I don't see why not. The snowplows should have all the roads open by this time."

"Maybe she's changed her mind about letting us see what's in there," Becky said.

"Oh, I don't think so," Felicia replied quickly. "She's our friend."

"I don't think it's going to make much difference

one way or another," Joan said. "If there ever was anything in that trunk, it's been picked clean."

They met just inside the front door after class that afternoon and made their way to Joan's convertible. They were a dozen steps away when Felicia stopped suddenly and pointed.

"Look, Joan!"

"At what?"

"You've had visitors."

Still, her best friend did not know what she meant.

"Somebody has been over to your car – a man by the looks of the tracks in the snow."

Joan started.

They hurried over to the red car and examined it carefully.

"There doesn't seem to be anything missing," Joan said.

"Maybe that's because there's usually nothing in it," Felicia said.

"It could be one of the men who followed us from Stilwell the other night," Becky said.

"Felicia doesn't think there was anybody following us home the other night," Joan said, scornfully. "She thinks it was all a big, fat dream."

"No, I don't." The Cartright girl got into the car and sat down. "I don't think that at all. I know there were a couple of men sitting in the car across the street while we were looking through Miss Delphina's trunk. And I know they started up about the same time we did. It does look suspicious, I've got to admit. And especially when we consider these tracks out to our car. But I can't help thinking that there's got to be a reason for things like that."

"That's simple. Somebody wants to stop us from going through Miss Morrow's trunk."

"But why?"

Joan stared at her blankly.

"You've got me. I can't come up with the remotest reason."

"I can't understand why anyone except us and Mrs. Graber would be interested in that old trunk."

"Neither can I."

"But that doesn't change my mind any. I *know* those men were following us. And I know that somebody prowled around my car."

* * *

Miss Delphina let them in the house in response to Becky's knock.

"You know the way to the attic," she said. "You don't mind if I don't go up with you, do you? It's such a hard climb for me."

"Not at all," Felicia told her quickly.

"I hope you finish going through that trunk soon," she said, a strange, unnatural tone in her voice. "I'm getting tired of having people run through my home all the time, and Timothy B is irritable and unhappy around strangers. I'm afraid you make him quite nervous."

"I didn't expect to have her say she's getting tired of us," Becky whispered. "I thought she liked to have us around."

"It's not Miss Delphina," Joan said, snickering. "It's Timothy B who's upset."

They went to the attic and got to work.

"In another afternoon or two, we ought to finish this job," Felicia said.

"If it takes that long," Joan broke in. "We're almost to the bottom of the trunk now."

"And we still haven't found anything that will be of help to Mrs. Graber in writing her book."

"What's more," Joan repeated, "I don't think there's anything in this trunk that'll help her, either."

"I–" Felicia's voice trailed away, and she looked up slowly.

"What is it?" Becky cried. "What did you find?"

For answer, Felicia extracted a small bundle of letters from the trunk.

"These were hidden in the lining," she said.

"Let me see them!" Joan exclaimed in a tense whisper.

"They sure look old," Becky observed.

"They are old. See how faded the ink is."

"Don't just look at them!" Joan said. "Open them."

Felicia's fingers trembled as she opened the first letter and scanned it.

"My dear Mr. Morrow:" Felicia read, stumbling over the faded handwriting. "I would be pleased to go to church with you Sunday night. You may call for me at seven thirty. Your friend, Elizabeth."

Joan snickered. "And you call that a love letter?"

"Maybe they'll get better as they go along," Becky said.

"The voice of experience."

"This one thanks him for a gift he gave her, so apparently there was a little progress."

"Here," Joan said, reaching for some of the letters. "At that rate, we'll be here all night. Let us read some of those."

They divided the letters and read for half an hour or so.

"Well," the Bailey girl said at last, "the letters are finally beginning to get a little more interesting. This one starts out, 'My dear Uriah.'" She chuckled to herself. "At that rate, they're about ten years from an engagement."

"Uriah?" Felicia echoed. "Isn't that the name of the Morrow who died and the church board wouldn't let the minister conduct the funeral?"

Becky nodded.

"But Elizabeth wasn't his wife's name. It was Amelia or something like that."

"That's the way I remember it," Felicia said.

"Maybe there was a scandal that caused the church

board to refuse to let his widow use the church for his funeral or bury him in the cemetery," Joan suggested.

"Or," Felicia went on, "this Elizabeth Haines might have just been a girlfriend of his. They could have gone together for a while and broken up."

"This letter doesn't sound as though they broke up," Joan said. "'My Darling: I count the hours since you were here. I count the hours until you will come back again. How wonderful it will be when this war is over, so we won't have to be apart any longer.' Now that is beginning to sound like a love letter."

There was a long painful silence.

"This must have happened before he was married," Becky observed at last. "This Elizabeth person doesn't sound like the kind who would carry on with a married man."

"It would be interesting to find out something about her, wouldn't it?"

Nobody answered the Cartright girl. After a moment or two, they went back to reading the letters again.

"I'm beginning to think that all the Morrows aren't as upright and straightforward as Miss Delphina would try to make us believe."

"What do you mean, Felicia?" Becky wanted to know.

"Listen to this. 'I was very proud when you joined General Washington's forces and went off to fight for our country, Uriah. I was proud to let people know you stood on the side of right and freedom. Lately, however, I have started hearing some very disturbing rumors. Please write and tell me they aren't true.'"

"Maybe she heard about Amelia," Joan murmured.

"He was in the army," Becky retorted. "He wouldn't have had time to hunt another girl."

Felicia read the letter once more silently.

"That could mean almost anything, I suppose," she said after a time. "But it sounds to me as though it may have something to do with the war."

"It sounds like that to me too," Becky said. "Maybe he was a coward."

"We'd have to know a lot more about it than we know now," Felicia said, "before we could even make a good guess as to what it's about. But I think we might be getting close to the sort of information Mrs. Graber can use in her book."

Joan got stiffly to her feet and rubbed her hip.

"I don't know about you," she said, "but I'm done. I've had it this afternoon."

"Maybe we should quit." Felicia started to put the letters back in the trunk.

"Why don't we take them home with us?" Joan said. "It'll be a lot more comfortable to read them there than it would here."

The Cartright girl held the letters thoughtfully.

"Miss Delphina did say we could take anything with us we wanted to."

She slipped the letters into her purse.

Miss Morrow was waiting for the girls in the living room, her wrinkled face ashen and her eyes dull and lifeless.

"Thank you so much," Felicia said.

"Did–did you get finished?" The older woman choked out the words.

"Almost. Another afternoon or two, and we should be through everything."

"I–I don't like to tell you this, but I–I don't think you'd better come here anymore."

The girls stared at her, eyes widening.

"But–"

"I know I told you it would be all right. And I don't like to go back on my word." Her frail hands were fluttering in agitation. "But Timothy B gets so upset when you're around that he sulks in his box most of the day. I–I think it would be much better if–if you wouldn't come here anymore."

She picked up a folded newspaper. It seemed to steady her trembling fingers.

"So–so please don't come back."

"We're terribly sorry if we've done something to offend you, Miss Delphina," Felicia told her tenderly.

The older woman started to speak, but checked herself. Her eyelids quivered. And she traced a small square hole in the newspaper with a nervous finger.

"You haven't offended me!" she blurted. "Now go away and leave me alone!"

Felicia held out her hand.

"We'll be praying for you," she said.

Miss Delphina choked.

Felicia and her friends left the little cottage and made their way back to Joan's car.

"That's the last thing I expected this afternoon," she said in a hushed voice. "Miss Delphina has always been so very friendly to us the other times we've come."

"I was never so surprised in my life," Becky observed. "When we went there this afternoon, she was as sweet as could be."

"This is what you call making a full circle," Joan said. "First she won't even let us in the house. Then she's as friendly and kind as somebody's grandmother and makes tea for us and everything. Now she chases us away and tells us not to come back."

"Maybe she is really as strange as she sounds sometimes when she gets to talking about her cat," Becky put in.

"I don't think so," Felicia countered loyally. "Miss Delphina is a very sweet old lady. It isn't like her to treat us the way she did."

"What do you mean?"

"Did you look closely at her while she was telling us not to come back?" the Cartright girl continued. "There were tears in her eyes."

"Maybe she was crying because Timothy B has been unhappy," Joan murmured.

"Joan! Be sensible!"

"I'm trying to be."

There was a long silence.

"Well," the Bailey girl said, "I guess that ends that. All of that work and the story of the Morrow family still won't be in Mrs. Graber's book."

They pulled into the dormitory parking lot and got out.

"I've still got these letters," Felicia said. "I should have left them with Miss Delphina."

"Now you'll have to take them back to her," Becky said.

"If you do, you're going alone," Joan informed her. "I know when I'm not welcome. Nobody has to hit me over the head with a baseball bat."

The girls hadn't noticed a dark sedan pull up to the curb and stop or a tall individual get out and approach them.

"You there!" a guttural voice exclaimed.

Joan screamed.

"Cut that out!" His hand snaked out and grasped her by the wrist. I ain't goin' to hurt you if you keep your mouths shut. I just got somethin' for you!"

Beady eyes darted from one frightened face to another.

"Which of you is Felicia Cartright?" he rasped.

"I–I am," she stammered.

"Here!"

He thrust an envelope into her hand and dashed away, disappearing into the darkness.

CHAPTER 7

THREATENING MESSAGE

Felicia and her companions stared at one another incredulously. An instant later, the dormitory door opened, and Miss Duncan flew to their sides. She was followed by half the girls in the lounge.

"Girls! Girls! Are you all right?"

"I–I think so." Felicia focused numbly on the envelope in her hand.

"What was it? What happened?"

"This man," Felicia began, gesturing weakly. "He came up to us and–and Joan screamed–"

Miss Duncan nodded her approval.

"That was most commendable, Joan," the dean said. "A Wellington girl is to maintain her dignity, but there are times when a good, healthy scream is called for."

She eyed the girls.

"And then what happened?"

"He grabbed me by the arm," Joan said, "and told us he wasn't going to hurt anybody. He just wanted to give Felicia something."

"So he shoved this envelope into my hands and ran away," the Cartright girl explained. "Then you and the others came running out."

Miss Duncan became aware of the girls who were crowded around them, listening curiously.

"I think we had better finish this discussion in my office," she said in an undertone. With that, she raised her head and clapped her hands sharply for attention. "Go back inside. All of you. The dinner buzzer will be sounding in a few minutes."

Miss Duncan said no more until they were in her office and had closed the door.

"May I see the envelope, Felicia?" she asked.

The girl handed it to her, and she opened it carefully. In spite of herself, she gasped.

"What is it, Miss Duncan?" Joan demanded.

"I think this is a matter for the police."

She sat down and dialed the number. While she was talking, Felicia picked up the piece of paper that had been in the envelope. The paper was from one of the narrow-lined tablets some people used for writing letters, and the words and letters had been clipped from a newspaper and pasted crudely in place.

"IF YOU KNOW WHAT'S GOOD FOR
YOU STAY AWAY FROM MISS MORROW!"

Felicia slowly laid the paper back on Miss Duncan's desk.

"That explains Miss Delphina today," she said. "She must have gotten a message like this too. She was warning us away because she didn't want us to get into trouble."

"But why?" Joan asked. "What would it matter to anyone that we dig into the story of the Morrow family?"

"I know it sounds crazy, but that must be the reason. It's the only thing it can be."

Miss Duncan hung up the phone.

"The police will be here in about an hour," she said crisply. "You had better go and eat. Then come back here and wait for them."

They started to leave.

"Don't say anything about this to the other girls."

"What should we say if they ask us about it?" Becky wanted to know.

"Refer them to me."

A few minutes before the hour was up, Felicia and Joan and Becky went back to Miss Duncan's office. The police were already there. They questioned the girls at length about the type of material they had been checking.

"It sounds to me like the work of a crank," one of the officers said at last. "We run into that sort of thing from time to time."

"Or some jokester," the other officer added. "Does

one of you girls have a boyfriend close by who might be capable of a trick like this – just to scare you?"

"My dear Mr. Collins," Miss Duncan broke in, "on occasion, Wellington girls have male escorts from acceptable backgrounds, but they do not have boyfriends. They are here to get an education, not to be thinking about boys."

Officer Collins grinned. "I've got three teen daughters myself."

"To answer your question, Officer," Felicia said, "we don't have any boyfriends."

The questioning went on for another half an hour or more.

"Well," Collins said finally, closing his notebook, "I think that gives us all the information we'll need. We'll get in touch with you if we are able to learn anything."

"Thank you," Miss Duncan replied.

"And if you see or hear anything strange, call us at once."

"We'll do that."

When the police were gone, the dean of women pivoted to face the girls.

"I'm sure Officer Collins is right about the note being the work of a crank," she said, "but as a precaution, I'm going to insist that you girls not be out after dark for the next two or three weeks and that you not go anywhere alone. If you have to run an errand, take somebody with you."

In their room, the girls continued to discuss the note.

"I suppose the police are right," Felicia said, "but I've got a funny feeling about all this."

"So do I," Joan retorted. "I get a funny feeling whenever I think about being messed up in it at all."

"Whoever wrote us that note got hold of Miss Delphina too," Becky put in. "I'm sure she'd never have talked to us the way she did."

Joan went over and sat down on the bed.

"There's got to be some sort of a tie with today for any of this to make sense."

"What do you mean?"

"There's got to be something at stake today that is affected – or might be affected by the material we're digging into right now."

Felicia sat down across from her.

"I don't see how that could be. All we found were a few old letters and a short reference to one member of the family in the church records."

The Bailey girl jerked upright.

"Maybe we haven't found it yet!" she exclaimed. "Maybe they just think we might find out something if we aren't frightened away."

"That could be." Becky drew in a deep breath. "But I'm like Felicia. I–" She stopped suddenly, eyes brightening. "Maybe the story is in the rest of those old letters you've got in your purse."

"I'd forgotten all about them." Felicia dug them out and opened one.

Becky and Joan crowded close, peering over her shoulder.

"There's nothing in that letter that would interest *anybody*," Becky said disappointedly.

It was the same with the next and the next and the next. Finally, they went through the last letter.

"Aren't there any more?" Joan asked.

"That's the last."

"There certainly wasn't anything helpful in those."

"You can say that again."

Joan kicked off her shoes.

"Let's talk about it tomorrow. Okay?"

"Sounds like a good idea."

Felicia was almost ready for bed when she stopped suddenly and turned to her roommates.

"The newspaper!" she exclaimed.

They stared at her, bewildered.

"Whatever are you talking about?" Joan asked.

"The newspaper Miss Delphina had in her hands when she told us that we weren't to come back anymore. I don't know why I didn't think of it before."

"Now wait a minute!" Joan exclaimed. "Back up and start over, will you? You lost me at the first turn."

"I just happened to remember," Felicia began, "that the newspaper she was holding had an item clipped out of it."

"I don't see what that has to do with it. A lot of

people clip things out of newspapers. It happens every day."

"I know it sounds crazy," Felicia continued, "but she did have it in her hand, and she was terribly upset. I thought there might be a connection between the two."

Joan's mouth firmed.

"I doubt it," she retorted, "but I suppose it wouldn't hurt to check it out – if we can think of some way to check out a thing like that."

"It shouldn't be too hard. All we've got to do is get copies of the daily papers that come into this area and read them."

"Only how are we going to find out what day's paper she was holding?" Joan asked. "People have been known to keep month-old newspapers around. Did you ever think of that?"

"Maybe they do, but they don't get upset at something they read in a month-old newspaper, that's for sure. I don't think we'll have to go back any farther than a week."

The next afternoon, the girls went to town and visited the drugstores and newsstands until they gathered copies of the daily papers that were circulated in the area.

"Some sort of a school assignment?" a clerk in the drugstore asked curiously.

"Not exactly."

"First time I ever had anybody come and want to

buy old newspapers. If you want many of them, I'll make you a real deal on them by the pound."

Joan snickered.

"Felicia's the mastermind behind this project. You'll have to talk to her."

"Thank you, no," Felicia answered. "This will be plenty."

They went back to the dorm, and after they had locked the door, they spread the papers out on the bed and began to go over them.

For an hour or more, they examined every item on every page of every newspaper they brought home.

"I'm beginning to think this wasn't such a good idea after all," Felicia said. In spite of herself, discouragement crept into her voice. "It does seem silly to expect to find something about the Revolutionary War in a paper printed now."

"That makes three of us with the same general idea, doesn't it, Becky?" Joan asked.

Becky did not answer her.

She was studying the paper before her.

"Miss Delphina had her paper folded to the want ad section," she mumbled to herself. "That would indicate that–" She chopped off the word.

"Girls! I've found it!"

Both Felicia and Joan crowded close to her.

"Listen to this! 'Urgent – before February 27. Must get in touch with the heirs of Lemuel G. Morrow, born

1760 or 1780, exact date illegible. Write to Edward, Box 14 c/o this newspaper, giving full particulars.'"

It was almost a minute before they could speak.

"It does sound interesting," Joan admitted. "I have to admit this is the very first thing that's sounded like a real, solid lead since we've been trying to work on this."

"I knew there was some connection between Miss Delphina getting upset and the research we've been doing," Felicia mumbled to herself. "I just knew it."

"What do we do now?" Becky wanted to know.

"We wait until morning, call the newspaper to find out who Edward is, and go see him," Felicia answered. "That's the quickest way I know of getting to the bottom of things."

Felicia and Becky slipped down to the phone in the lower corridor between classes the next morning, and Felicia dialed the newspaper office.

"I'm sorry," the man at the office said. "But we make it a policy not to reveal the names of those who place 'blind' ads with us."

"But we just want to talk with him," she replied. "We won't take more than five minutes of his time."

"I would suggest you write him a letter giving him your telephone number and explaining the nature of your request. We will forward it to him. It may be that he would call you immediately."

"Thanks." She did not try to hide her disappointment. "If we decide to do that, we'll write."

Becky was studying her face.

"It must have been bad news."

"He was sorry, but they don't give out that information. We have to write and see if this Edward what-ever-his-name-is answers our letter or calls us.

"What are we going to do now?"

"I don't know."

CHAPTER 8

SEARCH FOR LEMUEL

At noon, Felicia wrote a letter in answer to the ad, but she did not mail it immediately.

"We aren't heirs of this Lemuel Morrow ourselves," she said. "I can see this man taking one look at our letter and throwing it in the fireplace."

"We could write and tell him about Miss Delphina," Becky suggested. "That ought to be enough to cause him to investigate."

"What would we write him about her?" Felicia persisted. "I don't think there's really much that we could write about her and be honest. We don't know that she's a relative of this Lemuel Morrow. All we know is that they have the same last name. Edward could find that out by looking on the internet. He may have checked her out a long while ago."

"We know that somebody is trying to stop us from digging too deeply into the Morrow family past," Joan countered. "And that might be the reason for it. Miss Delphina could be a descendant of Lemuel Morrow."

"I feel the same as you do," she said, "but I think we've got to find some way of checking it out."

Felicia moved to the desk and picked up her Bible.

"You know," she said, "there was a family Bible in that trunk, and it had some names in it. Maybe we could get it and find out."

"Only Miss Delphina ordered us not to come back to her place," Joan replied. "Remember?"

"How could we forget?"

Becky folded the paper so the personal want ad was on top and read it to herself once more thoughtfully.

"Didn't that church record have all sorts of births and deaths listed in it?" she asked after a time.

Felicia and Joan stared at one another.

"That's it!" they cried in unison.

Becky eyed them blankly.

"What are you talking about?"

"The church records ought to trace the family from this Lemuel all the way down to Miss Delphina."

"If he was a member of that church," she countered. "You know, the ad didn't say anything about where he was supposed to have lived. Lemuel might be from some other place entirely."

"I'd never thought of that," Joan said.

"If he's one of Miss Delphina's ancestors, he went to church here," Felicia told them. "We've got her word for that. 'The Morrows *always* went to church in Stilwell. It's a family tradition.'"

"I guess you're right. She's left her name on the church rolls even though she isn't a Christian and doesn't want to be."

The girls wanted to go over to Stilwell and visit the neat white frame church on the edge of town, but they had outside reading to do that kept them busy Friday night and all day Saturday. In fact, it was Tuesday afternoon before they were able to go to the neighboring town.

The rector remembered the three girls but didn't seem particularly glad they had come.

"I'm very busy," he said. "Are you sure this information you want is in our records?"

"We're quite sure," Felicia told him. "And we know exactly what we want. It won't take us very long to look for it."

He hesitated briefly.

"All right." There was resignation in his voice. "But please get all the information you want today if you can."

As he brought out the records and laid them on the desk, he eyed the girls quizzically.

"A strange thing happened here last Friday night," he said. "A strange thing indeed. Somebody broke in here."

"They did!"

"I've been the rector here for more than forty

years, and it's the first time we've had a robbery." He paused. "If you can call it a robbery. Actually nothing was taken."

"I suppose you don't have much money around," Joan said, "especially at the end of the week. I mean, our church at home always banks on Monday morning. There's never any money in the church."

"That's just it. I did have quite a sizeable amount of money here in the safe in the study. We had a meeting on Thursday night and took up an offering for one of the denomination projects. But that money wasn't touched."

He started toward the door.

"I'm still a little shaken by that, I guess. So don't pay any attention to what I said about getting through with the records this afternoon. You can come back and look at them anytime you wish."

"Thank you."

Once he was gone, Joan leaned forward, speaking in tense, excited whispers.

"Doesn't that seem significant to you?" she asked fearfully.

"What?" Becky and Felicia asked.

"Miss Delphina was all shaken up and asked us to stay away from her place. We get a threatening note from a strange man telling us not to continue to pry into the history of the Morrow family. Now we come here to see if we can find proof that Miss Delphina is a descendant of Lemuel Morrow, and we find that the place has just been broken into, but no money has been taken."

"I suppose it could be a coincidence," Becky ventured.

"We'd better quit talking and get to work," Felicia said, "or the rector might change his mind about letting us see the church records and we'll be out of luck here."

They began to go through the musty, ink-written ledger item by item.

"Nothing in 1760," Joan announced, looking up.

"Nothing in 1780, either," Felicia added.

"Maybe there was an error and Lemuel was born sometime during the 1760s or the 1780s," the Bailey girl said.

"It won't take long to check."

"Wait a minute," Becky broke in. "You skipped a page, Felicia."

"No, I didn't."

"But you did. I was reading at the bottom of this page, and you must have turned two pages. What I was reading doesn't make sense. They must be parts of two different business meetings."

Felicia turned back. For a brief instant, her eyes widened.

"Girls!" she exclaimed in a taut whisper. "A whole sheet is missing!"

"There's a sheet missing here, too," Joan said. "We

jump from the middle of 1760 to the first quarterly business meeting of 1761."

Slowly Felicia placed both hands on the open book in front of her and raised her eyes.

"That's what those thieves were doing in here last Friday night!" she exclaimed numbly. "They tore pages out of this record book so nobody would find what we came looking for!"

Silence reigned except for the ticking of a large, old-fashioned clock on the wall.

"What are we going to do now?" Becky asked.

Felicia's lips pursed.

"Let me think." For a moment she closed her eyes.

"Do you suppose Miss Delphina would talk with us now?" Becky asked.

"She might."

"We could go and see her, and–"

"While you two are thinking, I'm going to look up something," Joan said, reaching for the record books.

"Now what?"

"I'm just curious to see what happened to Elizabeth Haines, that's all."

"If we just had a little more evidence before we go to Miss Delphina," Felicia said.

She got up and walked slowly to the study window. The sun was about to drop behind the western horizon. Long, narrow shadows from the old headstones in the church graveyard seemed to blend one with another and cast an eerie spell about the small, fenced enclosure.

"The answer to the riddle lies around here somewhere," she murmured. "If those stones could only talk!" Felicia jerked herself upright. "That's it!"

The sudden crescendo of her voice startled both Becky and Joan.

"What is it?" they cried. "What's the matter?"

"I know how we're going to find out about Lemuel!" she exclaimed, so excited she was trembling.

"Are you sure you feel all right?" Joan asked.

"You can laugh if you want to, but I know one record those thieves wouldn't think about destroying."

"What makes you so sure?"

"That's the way you started this particular wild goose chase," her friend reminded her. "It's worth a try, you say, so what do we do? We start trying – and about six weeks later, after working our poor little fingers to the bone, we realize it wasn't worth a try after all."

"Come on, Becky. We'll let her stay in here if she wants to." Felicia headed for the door. "If you don't want to be in on things, we'll just leave you where you are."

Felicia and Becky slipped on their coats and went down the church steps.

"What are we going to do, Felicia?" her companion asked, subconsciously lowering her voice.

The Cartright girl started to speak but stopped suddenly and grasped Becky's arm.

"What is it?" Becky croaked hoarsely.

"That car!" In spite of herself, Felicia almost pointed at the car that was moving slowly along the narrow road past the church.

"What about it?"

"It's the same one that followed us from Miss Delphina's the other night."

"Are you sure?"

"Positive!"

CHAPTER 9

TREACHEROUS SETBACK

Felicia pressed back into the shadows and pulled Becky with her.

"Wh-what do we do now?" her friend stammered.

"We're going back in the church for one thing. We're not going to stand out here and let those guys get hold of us again."

"Y-y-you don't think they'll c-c-come in, do you?" Becky asked.

Felicia shook her head.

"Not with the rector here. They'd be afraid to." They went back into the study. Joan looked up.

"Well," she said, "I suppose you've got it all solved and wrapped in a neat little package ready to deliver it to Miss Delphina and Mrs. Graber."

"Our friends are out here," Felicia broke in.

"Friends? What friends?"

"The ones in the black car that followed us!"

Joan's cheeks paled.

"Wh-what would they be doing out here?"

"What would they be doing threatening us the way they did?" Felicia asked. "And why would they scare poor Miss Delphina until she told us not to come to her place anymore? And why would they break into a church and tear certain pages out of old record books, pages that couldn't possibly have any value in themselves? There are a lot of questions that we don't have answers for."

"It doesn't make sense," Joan retorted practically. "None of it."

Becky shivered.

"But," she said, her voice thin with fear, "whatever is behind all of this, it must involve a lot of money or important people or something. If it didn't, they wouldn't go to all this trouble."

There was a brief silence.

"I did want to check the stones in the graveyard before we leave tonight," Felicia said, "but we don't dare do that now."

"At least something good's coming from this," Joan said cryptically. "It's keeping you out of a cemetery after dark."

Felicia made a face.

"You're as anxious to get to the bottom of this as Becky and I are."

"Speaking of getting to the bottom of things," Joan went on, "while you and Becky were getting half scared out of your wits, I got to the bottom of something that was bothering me a great deal."

"Now what?"

"I've been worried about Elizabeth Haines. I was afraid she had married Uriah Morrow in spite of everything and had been divorced or had pined away unloved and unmarried the way Miss Delphina is doing. But she didn't. She had more spunk than that. She went out and caught herself another guy."

"What was his name, Lemuel Morrow?"

"No such luck. She was married to Major Edward Curtis Benson."

"How interesting," Felicia said dryly.

"If you want something else that's interesting," Joan continued, "the name of the man who had the ad about Lemuel Morrow in the paper is also 'Edward.'"

"You aren't trying to tell us they're the same man, are you?"

"Just because I've come up with a clue of my own," Joan said with mock disappointment, "you don't have to get cute about it."

At that moment, the rector came to the door.

"Are you girls about finished for this afternoon?" he asked. "My wife and I are invited out to dinner this evening, and I really should be leaving."

"Yes," Felicia answered, smiling warmly. "I think we've finished."

He gathered up the record books.

"If you didn't find what you're looking for, you may come back another time," he said.

"Thank you, but I believe we've finished."

For some reason, he seemed to be quite relieved.

It was dark when the girls left the old church and drove back to town.

"At least the black car isn't following us this time," Becky said.

"At least we hope they aren't following us," Joan added, glancing uneasily in the rearview mirror.

They were almost back at school before anyone spoke again.

"I did a lot of kidding about all of this, but I would like to get to the bottom of it," Joan said finally.

"I think we all would," Felicia answered.

That night in their room, Becky brought up the subject of the men in the black sedan.

"Why do you suppose they drove by the church?" she asked.

"Probably to see if we obeyed their warning or not," Felicia replied.

"And they found out we didn't." Becky shivered in spite of the fact that the room was warm.

"Maybe if we stop now, they'll think they threw us off when they tore the pages out of the church records," Joan said. "If we quit, they'll leave us alone."

"That's exactly what I was thinking," Felicia replied.

Joan and Becky both stared at her.

"You don't mean that!"

A slow grin teased one corner of the Cartright girl's mouth.

"I didn't mean it exactly the way it sounded."

"I was afraid of that."

"What I was thinking was that we would try to give them the impression that we're quitting our search. Then they'll quit watching us so closely."

Joan's frown deepened.

"Now say that again, slowly."

"We'll make them think we're either afraid to look anymore or we're giving up."

"And just exactly how do you propose to do that?"

"They undoubtedly know by now that we stay here at school until after the last class in the afternoon," Felicia said. "We'll get permission to go out and look over that cemetery in the morning."

"She won't let us," Joan blurted. "I–I hope."

Felicia continued as though she didn't even hear her.

"If there's any connection between that ad in the paper and the missing church records, I believe the cemetery will show it. I doubt that they'd think to check the gravestones."

"You mean you think this Lemuel Morrow might be buried there?" Becky said.

"I think the Morrows might have a family plot in the cemetery. If they do and if there is a Lemuel Morrow buried there, we can go to Miss Delphina, show her the ad, and ask her for an explanation."

"As simple as that," Joan murmured.

"There's got to be an answer somewhere," Felicia exclaimed. "And we're bound to find it if we look long enough and in enough different places."

Becky crossed the floor and sat down.

"I can't help thinking about Miss Delphina," she said. "The only thing she has in the world is Timothy B. It's no wonder she fusses over him."

"And the pitiful thing is, she doesn't need to be that way."

"What do you mean?" Becky's eyes narrowed.

"She could trust Christ as her Savior," Felicia continued quietly. "Then she would not only go to heaven, but she would also have companionship here on earth. She would never be alone again."

"I still don't get it," the Strong girl replied curiously.

"The Bible says that Christ will never leave us or forsake us," she explained. "But that isn't all. If she were a Christian and would go to a good church, she'd find that people are eager to take her into their hearts. She'd find real enjoyment in others even though she is getting older and lives alone."

Becky turned Felicia's statements over in her mind.

"That's only part of what it means. When you accept Christ as your Savior, you have new direction and purpose in your life," Felicia explained.

"That's what I was thinking when you two were talking about Miss Delphina," Joan said. "All she has to think about is that stupid cat of hers. She's talked to him and cared for him so much she's half convinced herself that he's human. If she were a Christian and concerned about the things of the Lord, she wouldn't have time to make such a fool of herself over Timothy B. She'd be going to church and prayer meeting and would be occupying her time with reading her Bible and praying for missionaries and those who live around her who don't yet know Christ."

"That's right," Felicia broke in. "Miss Delphina's life could be so rich and full that she would be very happy. All she would have to do is to let Jesus Christ make it that way."

Becky sighed wistfully.

"I always thought of religion as just a means of getting to heaven," she said, "if I thought about it at all. But you make being Christian sound as though it's so much more than that."

"It is," both girls echoed. "It's much more than that."

There was a long silence.

"Being Christian is an entire way of life," Felicia continued, "not just religion. I don't see how anyone could even hope to be happy without Christ."

Becky's eyes gleamed, and, for a moment, her companions thought she was going to cry.

"You–you make me feel as though I'm missing out on the best part of life."

"You are," Joan said. "But you don't have to. You can make your decision for Christ right now."

The other girl breathed deeply.

"I don't know," she murmured. "I don't know whether I could ever become a Christian or not."

Felicia and Joan did not press her. However, that evening when they read the Bible together before going to bed, she came over and joined them. She sat on the side of the bed and listened intently.

CHAPTER 10

GRAVEYARD DISCOVERY

Felicia and her companions went to see Miss Duncan as soon as breakfast was over the following morning.

"I think this is a waste of time," Joan said under her breath. "Miss Duncan never let anyone skip class in her whole life."

"We'll soon know," Felicia answered.

They went into the office and requested permission to be gone that morning. She took off her glasses and, holding them by one bow, tapped her desk lightly.

"Just what do you think all of this has to do with getting material for Mrs. Graber's book?"

"Maybe a lot," Joan said. "Maybe nothing. The Morrow family is a very important family. They go all the way back to the Revolutionary Period."

"But we've been thinking about Miss Delphina too," Felicia said. "She's such a dear, sweet old lady.

And she must be in some sort of trouble. We've just got to help her."

Miss Duncan pursed her lips.

"Just so you don't get into trouble in the process," she said dryly.

The phone rang and she answered it. When she finished talking in a moment or two, she put her glasses back on, adjusted them carefully, and leaned forward.

"And you can't visit this cemetery after classes this afternoon?" she asked abruptly.

"We could," Felicia said, "but we think it would be much better to go during the morning. Because of the man who grabbed Joan in front of the dorm the other evening, I mean."

"I see." Miss Duncan opened a notebook on her desk and looked at it hurriedly. "I have nothing this morning that can't be canceled or postponed," she said. Her chair scraped on the floor as she got to her feet. "I'll go out to the cemetery with you. Then I'll *know* this unsavory individual will leave you alone."

They left the parking lot and drove across Wellington to the highway. In a few minutes, they were at the church and cemetery on the edge of Stilwell.

"Now what is this name we're looking for?" Miss Duncan demanded crisply.

"Lemuel Morrow," Becky told her.

The thin, crusted snow squeaked underfoot as they made their way to the iron gate.

"We'll each start in a different corner," Miss

Duncan said, "and take the quarter of the graveyard nearest us. That will make it possible for us to cover the entire cemetery in the shortest amount of time."

Felicia went to the far corner of the cemetery and began to examine the marble and slate headstones. The names were faded until they were all but illegible, and the dates went back to the time of the war against England for independence.

The cemetery was quite small, and it only took them a few minutes to go over it.

"No sign of Lemuel Morrow's grave," Joan announced as they came together.

"Another lead washed out," Becky said.

"I was so sure we'd find his grave here," Felicia said. "I'm disappointed."

"We found every other Morrow's grave except his," Miss Duncan said. "I do believe half of the stones here are for members of the Morrow family."

Felicia straightened.

"There's one missing," she said suddenly. "Uriah Morrow."

"But we know that grave isn't here," Joan countered. "The church records said so."

"I know that." She was looking around. "I was trying to figure out where they buried him."

"Perhaps they buried him on the family farm," Miss Duncan observed. "That is done on occasion."

"I heard of something else one time." Felicia left the others and started for the fence. "There was a cemetery where they refused to bury a person because he wasn't a member of the church. The people buried him just outside the fence."

Her companions frowned.

"I don't think there'd be a grave just outside this cemetery," Joan said.

"It won't take long to see."

Felicia went out the gate and started around the fence, examining the ground as carefully as possible under the thin coating of snow.

"Come, Joan – Becky," Miss Duncan ordered, "let's go around the other way." She noted the time. "If we hurry, we can check this out and be back to school in time for your next class."

"I knew it," Joan mumbled under her breath. "The leopard does not change her spots."

The dean of women pivoted.

"What did you say, Joan?"

The Bailey girl colored deeply. "I think it would be better if we both forget that I–I said anything."

"So do I." Miss Duncan's voice was stern, but there was a twinkle in her eyes.

Becky was half a dozen steps or so ahead of Joan and Miss Duncan. She turned at the corner and paused, kicking in the snow.

"Find something?" Felicia called to her curiously.

"I don't know. I don't think–" Her words trailed away. "There seems to be something here. It looks like a piece of cement or–"

Miss Duncan and Joan came up beside her.

"That isn't cement," the dean of women said, "it's an old gravestone that's been broken off and thrown out here."

"Let me see!" Felicia crouched beside it and dug at the snow with her gloved hand.

"There's a frost scraper for the windshield in the car," Joan suggested. "I'll get it."

Painstakingly, they scratched the snow from the weathered marble slab.

"It is an old gravestone!"

"Can you make out what it says?" Becky asked curiously.

Felicia bent closer.

"'In loving memory of Uriah Morrow, who passed this mortal life August 17, 1789, leaving his sorrowing wife, Amelia, and his baby son, Lemuel.'"

"There it is!" Joan cried. "Lemuel!"

"But that certainly doesn't tell us very much," Joan said.

"It tells us a great deal," Felicia countered. "It tells us that Miss Morrow is descended from Lemuel. And it tells us that there's a connection between her and the ad we found in the paper."

The girls looked at one another questioningly.

"What do we do now?" somebody asked.

"I think it's time for us to go and see Miss Delphina again," Felicia said.

"But she ordered us to stay away from her place," Becky said.

"That wasn't Miss Delphina talking. That was fear. She isn't that kind of a person."

Joan shrugged.

"I guess the worst that can happen is that she'll refuse to come to the door or tell us to leave."

They looked at Miss Duncan.

"Is it all right?" Felicia asked.

"We'll have to hurry," the dean said crisply. "We must be back at the school in time for lunch."

Joan stared at her.

"You see, Joan," she said so softly the other girls could not hear as they walked to the car, "a leopard can change its spots after all."

They drove into Stilwell and stopped in front of Miss Delphina's cottage. Felicia went to the door.

"I don't think she's going to get in," Becky observed.

"It doesn't look that way," Miss Duncan said. "Perhaps if I went–"

She got out and went briskly up the walk.

"No answer," Felicia said.

"Sometimes a brisk, authoritative knock will bring someone to the door when a less forceful approach will fail."

Still Miss Delphina did not respond.

"I don't think she's home," Felicia said.

"If she is, she has no intention of coming to the door."

"I don't think she would do that. She's not that kind."

"She wouldn't come in response to your knocking before," Miss Duncan reminded her.

"But that was before she knew us."

Miss Duncan rapped again and stepped back in resignation.

"It's no use, Felicia. We might just as well leave."

The girls had to go to class that afternoon, but, as soon as possible, they met in their room.

"What do you think we ought to do now?" Joan asked. "Write an answer to the want ad telling Edward about Miss Delphina?"

"I'd like to talk with her first."

"How can we talk with her? She won't let us in."

"Let's go out again," Felicia suggested, "just in case she wasn't home this morning."

Joan's eyes widened.

"Remember what happened to us the last time we went to see her?"

"We can take back those letters," Felicia said. "That'll be a good excuse for us to see her."

Joan sighed.

"All right. I guess we can go if you insist on it." She turned to Becky. "I'm going to warn you about something right now. If you run around with Felicia, you might just as well not argue with her. When she gets her mind set on doing something, you might just as well go along with it from the start. She's going to do it anyway."

Felicia made a face at her best friend.

Joan was going to stop in front of Miss Delphina's, but Felicia suggested that they drive around to the back.

"It won't be so easy for those men to see the car if they drive by," she said.

"You do come up with a good idea once in a while," Joan told her.

"I'm real handy that way."

Felicia went to the kitchen door and knocked.

No answer.

She knocked once more.

She was almost ready to leave when there was a sound of uncertain footsteps in the kitchen and the bolt on the door clicked metallically.

"Oh, it's you!" The old woman's voice brightened, and the door swung open. "I–I've been wanting to see you!"

The Cartright girl eyed her critically. The lines in Miss Delphina's face seemed to have deepened measurably since she last saw her. She had dark shadows under her watery eyes, and the tremor in her hands was much greater.

"Won't you come in?"

"Is it all right if Joan and Becky come in too?"

"By all means."

Miss Delphina limped into the living room and had them sit down.

"We were here to see you this morning," Felicia told her, "but you weren't at home."

"No, I–" Her voice choked momentarily. "I had to go to the store for some fresh meat for Timothy B."

"I see."

It was almost a minute before she could look at them again.

"I am so sorry I told you girls not to come back anymore," she said, "but I was so worked up over things that I felt I just had to be alone. I see now how silly that was of me."

Felicia's gaze met hers.

"Miss Delphina," she said, her voice soft and reassuring, "what is wrong?"

The older woman recoiled as though she had been slapped.

"Wh-what do you mean?"

"What is wrong?" Felicia repeated. "We'd like to help you if we can."

Fear glazed in Miss Delphina's eyes. Her trembling fingers flew to her throat.

"I think you'd better leave after all," she said hoarsely.

"But we only want to–"

"Don't you hear me?" the older woman's voice rose hysterically. "I want you to leave! Now!"

Numbly, the girls got to their feet.

"And don't come back!"

"I–I'm sorry," Felicia said.

She would have followed Joan and Becky out into the still, cold afternoon air, but Miss Delphina's bony fingers clamped on her arm.

"Wait!" she croaked.

CHAPTER 11

DIFFICULT CONFESSION

Felicia and her two companions stared at Miss Delphina incredulously.

"I've got to talk to you!" Emotion charged her voice until she could scarcely talk.

"Of course."

The girls went back into the kitchen, and the older woman turned to face them. For the space of a minute or two, she looked from one to the other.

"I–I haven't been able to sleep since I–I sent you away and t-t-told you not to come back."

Her voice choked until she could not speak. The girls eyed her, embarrassed by her anguish.

"All these years, I've been telling myself that I'm as good as any church member in Stilwell," she said, "that I hadn't sinned, so I didn't have any sin to confess." She swallowed the lump in her throat.

"I thought I was good enough on my own to go to heaven – that I didn't need to be saved."

She paused.

"The Bible tells us that none of us is good enough to go to heaven," Felicia said quietly.

"I–I found that out – in my own life, I mean." Her thin fingers were working nervously at her throat. "I lied to you girls," she blurted. "I've been lying to you all along. Will you forgive me?"

"Of course, we will," Felicia told her. "But that isn't the important thing right now."

"What do you mean?"

"Have you asked God to forgive you?"

She averted her eyes hesitantly and did not answer.

"We forgive you as though it never happened," the Cartright girl said. "But that is not enough. When we sin, we commit a bigger sin against God. That is why we must confess our sin and put our trust in Jesus Christ to save us. All of us are sinners and have earned the wages of sin, which is death."

Felicia opened her purse and took out her Bible.

"But I'm just a proud, lying old woman," Miss Delphina said. "I've been living a lie for the past forty years. God wouldn't want to save someone like me."

"God will save anyone who comes to Him in faith," Felicia reminded her.

Some of the strain left Miss Delphina's face. Still, she was not content.

"If I could only believe that."

"You can. It's in the Word of God," Joan put in, quoting John 3:16.

Miss Delphina stifled a sob.

"W-would you tell me how to be saved?" she asked brokenly.

They went into the living room and sat down. Felicia and Joan showed Miss Delphina what the Bible had to say about being converted.

"Yes," she acknowledged, "that's what I want for my life – or what there is left of it."

They knelt with her while she prayed, hesitantly asking God to forgive her sin and save her through Jesus Christ. Becky sat on the edge of her chair, listening intently.

* * *

"But I still haven't told you what I've done," Miss Delphina continued after half an hour or so, "or the ugly, proud individual I've been."

"You don't have to tell us," Felicia said. "God has forgiven you. That's all that matters."

But the gray-haired woman shook her head.

"No," she said, "I–I have to tell you. I lied to you. I have to make it right."

She was fighting desperately for self-control.

"Is it something that has to do with your ancestors?" Felicia asked quietly.

Miss Morrow nodded.

"My great-great-great-grandfather, Uriah Morrow," she said, jerking her head to indicate the painting on the wall behind her. "I've tried to pass him off as a hero. But he wasn't. I've known about him since I was a girl. I found Uriah Morrow's gravestone outside the cemetery and asked Papa about it. He wouldn't say anything, so I looked in the church records and found out the board wouldn't let him be buried in the graveyard. I knew, then, that there must be some big reason for it. I knew I shouldn't look any farther, but I couldn't quit. I had to keep hunting until I got to the bottom of it."

"What did you find?" Becky asked.

"His old discharge papers." A strange, hurt tone edged her voice. "I found out that he was dishonorably discharged. He was also convicted as a traitor and was going to be shot, but his life was spared by an order from General Washington."

"Oh, no!"

"How terrible!"

"No wonder the church wouldn't let him be buried in their graveyard," Joan said.

"Did you find out why?"

Miss Delphina shook her head.

"That's all I know, but–" Her voice trailed away. "I was so proud I burned his discharge and took his name off the painting. And when people asked me who it was, I lied so they wouldn't know the truth."

"We can understand how you felt," Felicia said. "And, after all, you didn't have anything to do with it."

"I've been so proud my family went back to the Revolutionary War I'd have died before I'd have let anyone know the truth. I even let myself get so mad at the church because of what they did to him that I quit attending." She stopped momentarily. When she began again, her lips curled in bitterness. "I'd give the rector a little money when he came to call once a year – because my name was Morrow and we were such an *illustrious* family, but I gave grudgingly. Not because I wanted to."

"But what does that have to do with us?" Joan asked.

Miss Delphina pulled herself erect from the couch where she had been sitting and hobbled over to the old-fashioned secretary in the corner.

"When this ad came out," she said, pointing to the newspaper clipping in her hand, "I–I was afraid you would find it or somebody else would learn of my connection with Uriah Morrow and the whole story would come out. I was trying to decide what to do the last afternoon you came to go through the trunk."

"I see," Felicia murmured.

"That was when these men came," she continued. "They warned me that if I didn't make you leave and not come back, they would see that you got the whole story about Uriah Morrow. They said our family name would be so blackened that the Stilwell officials would change the name of Morrow Street. And–and–" It was getting harder for her to go on. "And we Morrows would become a laughingstock all over the country."

She swallowed hard.

"I was so proud I thought that protecting the family name was the most important thing I could do."

"I knew there was some logical explanation for you telling us not to come back," Felicia said, smiling warmly. "I told the girls that you wouldn't do that unless you had a very good reason."

"There should never be a reason for telling friends not to come to see you," she answered.

"Why do you suppose those men were so interested in keeping us away from your place anyway?" Joan asked.

Miss Delphina frowned questioningly.

"That thought didn't occur to me before." She read the ad once more, slowly. "*Hmmmm,*" she murmured. "That's strange."

"What's strange?" Becky asked.

"This newspaper ad. I thought I'd read it carefully a hundred times, but it didn't register with me that there was a definite date on the ad. They wanted the information before February 27. That's the day after tomorrow."

"That's right." Felicia took the clipping and read it aloud. "And it says 'urgent.' I hadn't noticed that either."

"That makes it more of a mystery than ever," Joan observed.

Felicia drew in a long, deep breath.

"There's got to be some connection with today," she said. "Something that would make a lot of difference financially to somebody."

"Maybe another writer is working on a book and doesn't want Mrs. Graber to get the material in print first," Becky said.

At the mention of the book, Miss Delphina winced.

"It must be something that involves a lot more than the material for a book," Felicia replied.

Miss Delphina pursed her lips.

"I don't see how there could be any connection between Uriah Morrow and today," she said. "Amelia took little Lemuel to Pennsylvania after her husband died. There she married a widower by the name of Clinton. Lemuel's grandson (he would be my great-grandfather) moved back to Stilwell, where we Morrows have lived ever since." She shrugged her shoulders expressively. "There couldn't be any connection with today. If there was, I'd know about it."

There was a short silence.

"Are there any other families here in Stilwell who had ancestors in the war?"

She thought a moment.

"The Perrys moved to California three years ago," she mused, counting on her fingers. "Bill Farnsworth died last December. He was the last of their family.

And there's Edward Benson. His great-great-great-grandfather was Major Edward Benson, who was in charge of Company B that Uriah Morrow was in."

"Edward!" Joan cried. "Do you suppose he could be the Edward who is advertising for a descendant of Lemuel Morrow?"

"It couldn't be," Felicia broke in. "If he's lived here very long, he wouldn't have to advertise to find Miss Delphina. He'd already know about her."

The girls stared intently at the older woman. She moistened her lips uneasily.

"I–I have told people I wasn't a relative of Lemuel Morrow or his father, Uriah," she admitted. "I was ashamed to have them know the truth. I–I invented a relative by the name of Obed and had him in the war instead."

Felicia's forehead wrinkled thoughtfully.

"Why did you leave those letters in the trunk if you didn't want anybody to know that Uriah Morrow was a relative of yours?" she asked.

"Letters? What letters?"

"Didn't you know there were letters from one Elizabeth Haines to Uriah Morrow in the trunk?"

She shook her head. "If I had, I'd probably have destroyed them."

At last, the girls left Miss Delphina's house and drove back to the dormitory parking lot.

"What do you think we ought to do now?" Joan wanted to know.

"We could go to this Edward Benson and see if he's the one who placed the ad in the want ad section of the paper, but I'd like to find out a little more about his family first."

"So would I," Joan answered. "If you'll remember, I've been after you to check out Major Benson ever since we read in the church records that he married Elizabeth Haines."

"Then you ought to be very happy," Felicia said, winking at Becky.

Felicia, Joan, and Becky got permission to visit the local historical library that evening. The librarian on duty was the one who helped them when they went in to hunt for material at the start of the research.

"Hello." She smiled sweetly at them. "Still working, I see."

"Still working," Felicia told her.

"And what can I help you with this evening?" she asked.

"We'd like to see what you have on Major Edward Benson."

"Major Benson?" Her forehead creased. "Was he a Civil War officer?"

"Revolutionary," Joan said cryptically.

"Oh." Her manner changed almost imperceptibly. "I see."

She took half a step backward.

"I'll have to check the files. Would you please excuse me?"

She disappeared behind a row of bookshelves.

Joan turned to Felicia. "She isn't going to look for material on Major Benson," she said in a tense whisper.

"What makes you say that?"

"She knew the sort of research we were doing for one thing. She knew we weren't looking for any material on a Major Benson who fought in the Civil War."

"She could have made a mistake."

"And she didn't even go the right way to get a book on Major Benson for another. You two sit down and wait here. I'm going to see what this is all about."

Quietly Joan went the same general direction the librarian had gone. They had gotten to the library early and there was no one else in the rooms except them and the librarian.

Joan made her way around the end of two long shelves of books and into the next room, looking down each aisle. The librarian was not in sight.

Strange she could disappear so quickly, the Bailey girl thought to herself. *Maybe she went to call her boyfriend or take care of something urgent she just remembered.*

Joan was about to turn back to Felicia and Becky when she heard the guarded tones of somebody talking on the telephone. Somebody who didn't want to be overheard.

As soon as Joan realized the librarian was on the

phone, she started to back away but not in time to keep from hearing.

"Mr. Benson?" the librarian asked softly. "I thought you would want to know that they're back again. This time they're asking about material on Major Edward Benson."

Joan caught her breath sharply.

The librarian had called this Mr. Benson to tell him about them!

CHAPTER 12

TRUTH REVEALED

Joan pivoted and hurried back to where Felicia and Becky were waiting.

"Come on," she whispered frantically. "We've got to get out of here!"

"Why?" Becky asked. "What's wrong?"

"I can't tell you now, but we've got to go." Her face was ashen, and her breath was coming in short, quick stabs.

Felicia stood.

"All right," she said, "but not before we get the books we came here to get."

Joan glanced uneasily over her shoulder in the direction from which she had just come.

"Okay, but hurry."

"What happened to the librarian?" Felicia asked. "I thought she was going to get the books for us."

"Don't wait for-" Joan stopped suddenly as she

saw the tall, angular lady who was taking care of the library coming toward them from the far end of the room.

"I'm sorry to keep you waiting," she said, smiling apologetically. "Now, who was it you wanted information on?"

"Major Edward Benson."

"Major Benson." Her lips tightened. "Oh, yes. I'm not sure whether we have anything on the major or not."

"You've got some books on Major Benson," Joan retorted. "There's a whole raft of them. I remember seeing them the last time we were here."

"Are you sure?" The librarian's face colored delicately.

"They're right here." Joan went over to a nearby shelf and pulled a couple of books from it. "*The Journal of Major Edward Benson. The Military Tactics of Major Edward Benson. Illustrious Family: The Story of the Bensons.*"

The librarian managed a weak smile.

"Of course. I don't know what's the matter with me. We have so little call for them that I had completely forgotten about them. I should have checked the files before I spoke."

"We'd like to check these out."

"Oh, I'm sorry." Her smile came back again, a bleak, wisp of a smile that could just be read on her lips. "I'm sorry, but we don't allow those books to be checked out. You'll have to arrange to do your research here."

"Don't you remember the letter we showed you from the officers of the Historical Society?" Felicia broke in. Even as she spoke, she was fishing in her purse for it. "Mrs. Graber went to them and got special permission for us to check out anything we wish."

The librarian took the letter and read it over slowly.

"This is irregular," she said primly. "Most irregular."

"Mrs. Graber said the Historical Society president told her it is something that's often done when responsible people are researching some special project," Joan broke in.

By this time, the librarian's cheeks were scarlet.

"Well, I guess there's nothing I can do except let you take them," she said reluctantly.

The girls picked up the books and started to leave the library.

"Let's go out this door." Joan indicated the side entrance.

"But the car's out front."

"Let's go this way just the same."

Felicia and Becky followed her.

"Now what was that all about?" the Cartright girl demanded when they were on the sidewalk.

Hurriedly Joan told them what she had overheard. "I don't know whether that black car is out front yet or not, but it's going to be. You can bet on that," she concluded.

"So what do we do now? We've still got to go out to the car. He's going to see us then."

"The car can stay right where it is until tomorrow morning." Joan said. "We'll walk home."

"I get it," Becky exclaimed. "Our Mr. Benson will think we're still inside, and he'll be waiting for us."

"If his librarian friend doesn't call him," Joan said.

They hurried along the street at a pace little short of running.

"Y-you're going to have to slow down," Becky said, panting heavily. "I don't think I can go another step."

"A Wellington girl never quits," Felicia told her.

"Besides," Joan added, "you've got all night to get rested up once we get back to the dorm."

"If I ever get out of this, I don't think I'll ever run around with you two again," Becky murmured.

"That's what I used to say about Felicia."

"Don't you ever believe it, Becky. Joan's the one who gets us into all this trouble."

They were nearing the campus of Wellington School for Girls when the black sedan turned the corner.

Becky saw it first.

"Girls!" she cried. "It's that man again!"

They broke into a dead run.

As soon as the driver of the car spied them, he speeded up, slammed on the brakes as he neared them, and jumped out.

"He's coming!" Joan shouted.

Half a dozen steps from the dorm, he grabbed Felicia by the arm and spun her around.

She struggled to jerk away.

"Oh, no, you don't!" he snarled. "Give me those books!"

Felicia swung her arm savagely and cracked him in the face with the thick volume she was carrying.

"Ouch!" He let go of her and staggered back.

Joan and Becky pounced on him, kicking him in the shins and flailing him with their purses and the books they were carrying.

"Help!" he cried, trying to get away. "Help! Help!"

At last, he broke free of them and went dashing across the grass.

"Are you all right, Felicia?" Becky asked, going over to her.

"I think so." She was panting heavily.

At that moment, Miss Duncan came hurrying out.

"Girls!" she cried. "What's wrong?"

They watched the dark figure jump into the car and speed away.

"Nothing," Felicia said firmly. "Everything's under control."

Miss Duncan took them inside and questioned them carefully.

"That settles it," she said when they finished telling her what had taken place that evening. "In the morning, I'm going with you. We'll pick up Miss Delphina, go down to Edward Benson's office, and have this out with him. This affair has gone quite far enough."

At last, the girls were able to go up to their room.

"I don't know whether I want to go over to Edward Benson's or not," Becky said.

"I do," Joan retorted. "I want to get to the bottom of this."

"So do I," Felicia said. "But I think the answers are here." She tapped the books about Major Benson with her forefinger.

"What makes you so sure?"

"He was so anxious to keep them out of our hands for one thing."

Joan snickered. "He sure changed his mind about that."

Felicia picked up Major Benson's journal.

"We've got a lot of reading to do if we're going to go through these books tonight."

"You can say that again."

Becky curled up on her bed with *The Military Tactics of Major Benson*. Felicia took the journal, while Joan read the book about the family. It was almost an hour before any of them spoke.

"The major really fell for Elizabeth Haines," Joan said finally. "The author says he was sick for a time after she chose Uriah Morrow over him."

"Then what happened?" Felicia asked.

"I don't know. I haven't read that far yet."

There was a brief silence.

"I didn't know they were rivals for her," the Cartright girl said thoughtfully. "Did you?"

"Those letters to Uriah certainly didn't sound like it."

"I wonder what happened to cause her to jilt Uriah Morrow and take Major Benson."

"Maybe you'd find out if you'd trade books with me," Becky suggested.

"Military tactics?" Joan queried, her lips curling distastefully. "You must be kidding."

"I think we ought to trade books for a while," Becky went on. "All I know about military tactics is that soldiers use guns."

"We would trade with you, Becky, but we wouldn't want to ask you to make such a sacrifice."

"I wouldn't mind that at all. I'd even let you read about his most thrilling victory."

"Is there one of those?"

"Oh my, yes. It was so important it may have shortened the war."

Felicia's voice grew serious.

"That must be the one I was reading about in here. He surprised the British at Cooper's Ferry, split their force in two, and cut the main supply route to the south."

"That's the one. Want to hear what it says in here?"

"No, thanks," Joan protested.

"Well, you're going to hear it anyway. If I have to read it all, the least you can do is listen to part of it.

'Major Benson's source of intelligence for the Cooper's Ferry Battle was superb, although never revealed. He knew exactly how large the enemy forces were and how they were deployed.'"

"How thrilling! Read us more."

"'Among the British captives was an American deserter who was tried for treason and–'"

"That's enough!" Joan threw both hands in the air. "I give up!"

But Felicia was interested.

"Read that again, Becky."

"About the British captives?" she asked.

"About the American who was tried for treason."

"All it says is that a court-martial found him guilty and sentenced him to death, but the sentence was commuted to a dishonorable discharge."

"Do you suppose that could be Uriah Morrow?"

Felicia's face wrinkled thoughtfully. "I suppose it could be," she said. "That's what happened to him."

"That could explain a lot of things," Joan said. "It could explain why Elizabeth's letters to Uriah began to cool. And if he showed himself to be a traitor and the major was a big hero, it would explain why she dumped her fiancé and picked another."

"It does fit," Felicia said, "but that's about all we can say. We don't really know for sure."

They went back to reading.

"He tells about the trial of the deserter in his journal," Felicia said a little later.

"Does he give his name?" Joan asked.

She shook her head. "All he says is that he was ill and confined to his quarters at the time of his trial."

"And I was all set for the name of the deserter," Joan said.

The next morning as soon as breakfast was over, Miss Duncan took the girls to downtown Stilwell.

"Are we going to stop and pick up Miss Delphina?" Felicia asked.

The dean of women shook her head.

"Mrs. Graber is going to bring her. We're to meet them at Mr. Benson's office."

When they reached the law office of Benson and Benson, Mrs. Graber and Delphina were already there.

"I'm happy to have you ladies come to see me," Mr. Benson said, smiling. He was a slender, gray-haired man a little older than Miss Duncan. "What can I do for you?"

"You're not the one!" Joan blurted.

"What do you mean?" he asked curiously.

"You're not the man who has been chasing us all over!"

His smile broadened.

"I am an eligible bachelor," he said. "And I don't think anyone would blame me for chasing such attractive young ladies, but I'm not guilty this time."

Miss Duncan spoke up. "Are you the one who placed this ad asking for information about the descendants of Lemuel Morrow in the paper?"

He nodded.

"I am. Now may I ask you a question? Why are you concerned about it?"

"Tell him, Felicia."

The Cartright girl started at the beginning and told him everything that had taken place.

"I don't blame you for being upset." His eyes narrowed. "I'll see that it doesn't happen again."

"Then you know who it is?"

"I think so. I have two second cousins who think they stand to inherit a considerable amount of money from me if I don't find the descendants of Lemuel Morrow. What they don't know is that they've been wasting their time. I cut them out of my will a year ago."

"And now you've found a descendant of Lemuel Morrow," Miss Duncan reminded him.

"And I'm disturbed at you, Delphina. I went to you first, and you denied ever hearing the name."

"I was a silly old fool."

"Do you mind telling us what this is all about?" Joan asked.

"I don't rightly know," he said. "I'm something of a history buff myself. I was snooping around in some things my dad and his dad and granddad had collected when I came across a copy of Major Benson's will. He left a sizeable amount of money to Lemuel Morrow or his heirs."

"That's strange," the Wellington dean of women exclaimed.

"Did he say why?" Felicia asked.

The attorney shook his head. "No, but the wording gave me the distinct impression that it was to right a great wrong. But Lemuel Morrow had left and nobody could locate him, so the bequest was never made."

"I see."

"I've been doing a lot of thinking about it since I found the will. I don't know why he was going to leave the money to the Morrow family, but I thought I ought to find Lemuel's heirs if I could and take care of it for him."

Felicia jerked upright. "Do you have a Bible here?"

"Yes, why?"

"I just thought of something." She laid down the journal and opened the Bible. "Look at the last entry in the journal, Mr. Benson," she said.

He read it aloud. "'My name is Edward, but it should have been David.' You know, I've puzzled over that more than once, but I never could figure it out."

"Listen to this," Felicia went on. "'Set Uriah in the forefront of the hardest battle.'"

"That's it!" Joan cried excitedly. "Why didn't we think of it before? Uriah Morrow was the American soldier who pretended to desert to the British in order to furnish the major with the information he needed to fight successfully against them. The major probably didn't plan it that way, but when Uriah was captured as a deserter, he let him stand court-martial because of his own love for Elizabeth Haines."

"That couldn't be!" Miss Delphina broke in. "I've read the major's journal half a dozen times. He was an honorable, courageous man."

"So was David," Edward Benson said quietly. "This clears up many things that I've wondered about for a long time." He turned to Miss Delphina. "Delphina, I'm going to make up this injustice to you in the only way the major felt he could make it up to your family. I'm going to see that you are mentioned liberally in my will."

She snorted her indignation.

"And me twenty years older than you are? How silly can you get?"

"Then I'll give it to your favorite charity."

Her eyes brightened.

"The Wellington School for Girls?" she asked.

"If you wish." He wrote down the name. "And, of course, I'll release the story to the papers to clear your family name."

"No, Edward." Miss Delphina laid a work-worn hand on his arm. "The major was a great man who did much for our country. Let's not destroy his memory now."

His gaze met hers.

"That doesn't sound like the proud Miss Delphina I used to know."

"It's not." She smiled. "This is Delphina Morrow, the sinner who is saved because of Jesus's love for her."

"Praise the Lord!" He thrust out his hand impulsively. "I won't release the story to the papers if you'd rather I didn't," he said a moment later. "But I'm going to insist that Mrs. Graber use the account in full in her book."

"Thanks to the girls, I now have material enough to make a book," Mrs. Graber put in.

Mr. Benson followed them to the door of his office as they went to leave.

"Miss Duncan?"

"Yes?" She turned back, coloring delicately.

"If you aren't going to be doing anything this evening, I would like you to have dinner with me if you care to. We can talk about this legacy for the school over prime ribs or steak."

"Oh–" Her voice fluttered. "I'd love to."

THE
FELICIA CARTRIGHT
SERIES

Felicia Cartright, a petite blonde who is one of the most popular students at Wellington School for Girls, has a surprising inclination toward mysteries. If a mysterious situation arises, it either makes its way to Felicia, or Felicia somehow finds it. Though this is a bit trying for her happy-go-lucky roommate, Joan Bailey, it does prevent life from becoming monotonous. It also enables Bernard Palmer, the popular author of the "Danny Orlis" books, to write an entertaining series of stories for girls aged twelve to eighteen.

The mysteries range from a valuable missing antique to an attempt by claim jumpers to steal a deposit of tungsten ore. There's excitement and action galore—but there's also spiritual guidance and blessing because Felicia and her partner-in-adventure love the Lord and take Him into account in all their experiences.

AVAILABLE FROM WWW.ANEKOPRESS.COM